Amish Values
for Your Family

Books by Suzanne Woods Fisher

Amish Peace: Simple Wisdom for a Complicated World
Amish Proverbs: Words of Wisdom from the Simple Life
Amish Values for Your Family: What We Can Learn
from the Simple Life

LANCASTER COUNTY SECRETS
The Choice
The Waiting
The Search
A Lancaster County Christmas (September 2011)

Amish Values
for Your Family

What We Can Learn
from the Simple Life

Suzanne Woods Fisher

R Revell
a division of Baker Publishing Group
Grand Rapids, Michigan

© 2011 by Suzanne Woods Fisher

Published by Revell
a division of Baker Publishing Group
P.O. Box 6287, Grand Rapids, MI 49516-6287
www.revellbooks.com

Printed in the United States of America

Library of Congress Cataloging-in-Publication Data
Fisher, Suzanne Woods.
    Amish values for your family : what we can learn from the simple life / Suzanne Woods Fisher.
        p.   cm.
    Includes bibliographical references.
    ISBN 978-0-8007-1996-8 (pbk.)
    1. Conduct of life. 2. Families. 3. Amish—Conduct of life. 4. Aphorisms and apothegms. I. Title.
BJ1581.2.F554 2011
241′.0497—dc22   2011013313

Scripture quotations labeled NIV are from the Holy Bible, New International Version®. NIV®. Copyright © 1973, 1978, 1984 by Biblica, Inc.™ Used by permission of Zondervan. All rights reserved worldwide. www.zondervan.com

Scripture quotations marked KJV are from the King James Version of the Bible.

Scripture quotations marked NKJV are from the New King James Version. Copyright © 1982 by Thomas Nelson, Inc. Used by permission. All rights reserved.

To protect the privacy of those who have shared their stories with the author, some details and names have been changed.

Published in association with Joyce Hart of Hartline Literary Agency, LLC

11 12 13 14 15 16 17   7 6 5 4 3 2 1

This book is dedicated to the next generation in my family, which started with Blake, who was born as I wrote this book. I am hoping for many grandbabies more to come. May each one of you keep the candle of faith well-lit and passed on.

> One generation will commend your works to another; they will tell of your mighty acts.
>
> Psalm 145:4 NIV

Contents

Contents

Acknowledgments

The Budget is a weekly newspaper for the Amish-Mennonite community, published in Sugarcreek, Ohio, since 1890. A scribe from each district sends in a weekly (more or less) letter that summarizes community news: who was born, who died, and all of life in between. When I first began this project, editor Keith Rathbun graciously gave me permission to include excerpts from *Budget* letters that shed light on the Amish: their family life, their work, their rich sense of humor, and their dedication to faith and church. Many scribes end letters with a saying or proverb. Most of the proverbs included in this book are from *Budget* scribes. I read the *Budget* regularly to study the Amish life—how the year's seasons shape the farm, the variety of occupations the Amish are involved in, the values they believe in. Always, always, they point to God's sovereignty. Great thanks and appreciation to the *Budget* scribes who chronicle their lives for others to enjoy.

I also want to thank Mary Ann Kinsinger for sharing particular stories from her blog, *A Joyful Chaos*, to round out this book so nicely.

Acknowledgments

My thanks to a few special Amish families in Lancaster County who shared their lives and opened their hearts, offering me the gift of a lovely friendship. And to my favorite traveling buddy, Nyna Dolby, for her ready camera and copious notetaking!

My everlasting gratitude goes to my agent, Joyce Hart, and my editors, Andrea Doering and Barb Barnes, for giving me the opportunity to write for Revell. To the wonderful staff of Baker Publishing Group, who put such attention-to-detail into each and every book, you are simply the best.

Last but always first, thank you to the Lord Almighty for letting me write for his glory.

Introduction

The Disappearing Childhood

The kind of ancestors you have is not as important as the ones your children have.

Amish Proverb

Not long ago, I was asked to speak to a young mothers' group. The topic focused on incorporating some Amish child-rearing values into today's modern families without "going Amish." Later, a woman approached me to share a story. Attached like Velcro to her knee was a two-year-old girl, her curly-haired daughter. "Just last week," this woman said, "a friend told me that I really need to have more scheduled activities for my little girl. We do attend a Gymboree class once a week, but that's not enough, this friend said. She thinks I should sign my daughter up for soccer."

Soccer? For *two-year-olds*? They haven't even learned to count yet. How do they even keep score?

On the drive home, I mulled over the conversation with that young mom—a window into the kind of stress families are facing.

Over-the-top pressure to be a success! This mom had been a college soccer player, so there was a part of her that wondered if her daughter might have a better shot at an athletic scholarship someday if she started now. But there's a cost to that logic—a "disappearing childhood."

Studies are finding some alarming trends in modern American families. In the past twenty years:

- children's free time has declined by twelve hours a week;
- time spent on structured sports activities has doubled;
- family dinners are down by a third; and
- the number of families taking vacations together has decreased by 28 percent.

Additionally, parents now spend 40 percent less time with their kids than they did thirty years ago (that statistic *includes* driving in the car), and a 2009 study by the Annenberg Center at the University of Southern California found that the higher the income, the less time an American family spends together.[1]

The decline in family time, this study found, coincided with a rise in internet use and the popularity of social networks. Whether it's around the dinner table or just in front of the TV, American families are spending less time together.

Let's contrast those alarming trends to the Amish, who maintain one of the strongest and most stable family systems in America. New studies are finding that major depression occurs only one-fifth to one-tenth as often among Amish as it does among the rest of the US population. The Amish have close to a zero percent divorce rate. Harvard School of Medicine recently found that Amish people have a much lower rate of heart disease than do average Americans. Another new study found that they have lower rates of cancer.

Few people are aware that the Amish are the fastest-growing population in the United States. In 1900, there were five thousand Old Order Amish in America. Sociologists assumed they would assimilate into the wider culture. Yet by 2008, according to Donald B. Kraybill, Senior Fellow at the Young Center for Anabaptist & Pietist Studies at Elizabethtown College, there were over 233,000 Old Order Amish. And half the population is under eighteen. The growth is coming from large families, with an 85 to 90 percent retention rate as children become baptized into the church as young adults.

The Amish seem to be doing something right.

So should we all "go Amish"? Of course not! However, there is much we can learn from these gentle people about raising our families well: to help prioritize what's truly important, to simplify decision making, to slow down as a family, to safeguard time together, and when age-appropriate, to let go. *Amish Values for Your Family* invites you into Amish farmhouses for a hearty meal, to explore the topic of rearing children who are "in the world but not of it."

So grab a cup of hot coffee, put up your feet, and come inside the Amish world with me.

Section One

Children Are Loved but Not Adored

The best things in life are not things.

Amish Proverb

Whenever I speak to a group about the Amish, there is a moment when the audience stills, leans forward in their chairs, and begins to scribble notes. It happens when I make this statement: "Amish children are loved but not adored."

The Amish view children very differently than we do. They love and value each child—in many ways, they value marriage and family *more* than the non-Amish do. They consider each child to be a gift from God. The average family has six or seven children. Ten or more is not unusual! Children with physical or mental handicaps are thought of as "special children." I've heard quite a few Amish parents of handicapped children comment on how much they've learned from the gift of this "special child."

The main career focus of couples is to raise children to love God and to remain in the Amish church. The first thing an Amish child begins to learn is that there is always a higher authority to yield to—parents, older siblings, church, and God. But Amish parents believe a child belongs to God, *not* to them. Such a perspective allows parents to raise their children with clear boundaries and a healthy detachment. Hoped for, wanted, loved . . . but not adored. As a result, children are always involved in the life of the family—but it does not *revolve* around them.

Few would disagree that an Amish childhood is a special one. The best of all, perhaps. Secure, safe, enveloped in family and meaningful traditions. Even those who have left the church reflect on their childhood with fond, wistful memories. Raised in rural settings, Amish children have remarkable freedom—the run of the farm with very little supervision (or so they think!)—with time to play, to explore, to be kids. "We weren't plugged into a TV or an iPod," said one Amish farmer in Ohio. "We relied on our imaginations."

So as I was doing interviews for this book, I asked my Amish or formerly Amish friends this question: What made your childhood so special?

Here are some responses to that question, in their own words:

"The amount of quality time a family spends together. I was one of thirteen kids. My family had a dairy of sixty cows, and we milked them all by hand, twice a day. I remember being only three or four years old and having the job of holding the cow's manure-caked tail so it wouldn't hit my dad's face as he milked. We would sing songs while we milked—gospel songs, all kinds of songs—in the quiet of that barn."

—Mose Gingerich, raised in an Old Order
Amish family in Wisconsin

"I would have to say it's because we were involved in everything. We worked alongside our parents; we always felt like we were needed and appreciated."

—Mary Ann Kinsinger, raised Old Order Amish
in Somerset, Pennsylvania; writes
a blog about her childhood

"We had a farm. Dad was at home. We were all together, out in the country. We were taught a wonderful work ethic. I appreciate it all the more the older I get. It's a real blessing if you're taught to work even if you don't get paid. And finally, I think growing up in a godly home makes an Amish childhood special. Of course, some homes are more godly than others. But I cherished my godly upbringing."

—Barbara Weaver, Old Order Amish
raised in Napanee, Indiana

"The quiet. I remember being out in the barn where there was absolute quiet. No radios, no cars, no nothing. Just the sound of the cows lulling and the horses stamping their hooves in their stalls."

—Eli Beachey, Old Order Amish raised in
Adams County, Indiana

"There's a oneness in the home among the Amish. Mom and Dad were home. Children were the priority. I know it might not be possible in today's families to have that. It seems as if they need to have two incomes. But it's the best thing I can think of about being Amish—Mom and Dad were home."

Monk Troyer, whose father was a minister
in an Old Order Amish church

Time together as a family. Time with Mom and Dad. Time without electronic distractions. Time to be a child, to play, to learn skills, to explore the natural world. The Amish have a saying: "The best thing you can spend on your children is time." Just . . . time.

The Rabbit Hutch

A family that works together, grows together.

Amish Proverb

The closest neighbor to the Tom Weavers, a large Amish family in Goshen, Indiana, is the Johnsons, a small English (non-Amish) family. Although they were both farming families, they didn't interact much other than to nod and wave—until a winter night when the Weavers needed to get ten-year-old Will to the hospital with a bout of appendicitis. The Johnsons dropped everything and drove Will and his parents to the hospital. Trevor Johnson, age eight, went along with his parents to the hospital each day to visit Will. Those hospital trips broke down a barrier, and soon the families felt comfortable asking for favors from each other. Trevor and Will became fast friends.

The following summer, Will was given two pet rabbits by a cousin. Will and his dad went right to work to build a hutch. They spent a hot August day buying materials, sawing wood, and nailing wire screen in place. Will worked right alongside his father, Tom—his small hands covered by his father's large ones—sawing, hammering, sanding. By evening, the hutch was ready for his rabbits.

Trevor and his dad, Peter, came across the yard to see the finished hutch. "How much did you spend on that, Tom?" Peter asked. When Tom told him the price of supplies, Peter scoffed. "Would've cost half that to just buy it at the feed store. They're on sale down there."

"We looked at those," Tom said. "They aren't made to last."

"The hinges were cheap," Will said. "The doors didn't even close tight."

"You could have bought two for that price," Peter said. "Use one for a year or so, then toss it and use the next one. Assuming, of course, Will still has an interest in the rabbits."

In his gentle way, Tom said, "Oh, he'll still have an interest. He's planning to make a business out of breeding rabbits."

Peter shrugged. "Well, kids start a lot of things and lose interest."

"Maybe Trevor could have one of my rabbits after I have my kits," Will offered.

Trevor's eyes lit up. "Yea, Dad! Maybe we could build a hutch!"

"We can buy a hutch, you mean," Peter said. "No reason to reinvent the wheel."

"Unless you're trying to teach your son how to use a hammer and saw," Tom said. "Unless you want to give your son skills he can use for a lifetime. And you're trying to teach him to build things that last. To take pleasure in his work. Unless you don't mind missing those good talks a father and son have while they're working together, side by side." Tom packed up the tools. "If you don't mind missing those things, then, sure, you can just buy the hutch down at the feed store."

Road Map: Getting There from Here

When you find yourself thinking, "It would be easier to buy such-and-such than to make it," slow down for a moment. Ask yourself what is more important—to check it off the list? Or to use the opportunity to do it yourself and teach skills to your child?

What special skills do you have? How did you develop them? Most likely, some adult in your life taught you with patience and perseverance. Consider the skills you'd like to pass on to your children. One Rhode Island family devotes Sunday afternoon to cooking a large meal. An Arkansas family spends one Saturday a month hiking new trails. Today, make a plan to teach your child something new. Cooking, carpentry, or a dynamite tennis serve—it won't happen without a plan. You're giving your children more than time, skills, and memories—you're teaching them how to be lifelong learners.

In their own words . . .

Three-year-old Kyle likes to sing. His favorite song is "My God is so big, so strong and so mighty; there's nothing my God cannot do." His mother listened as he walked around the house singing; she was having trouble understanding the last phrase since something didn't sound right. Finally, she had it! "My God is so big, so strong and so mighty; and I don't know what to do."

—Scribe from Spooner, Wisconsin

The Mud Hole

Keeping a neat house is like threading beads on a string with no knot on it.

Amish Proverb

O n a rainy summer morning, Hannah Miller watched from the upstairs window as her husband, Marlin, handed shovels to their three young sons—aged 4, 5, and 7. Marlin had a booming voice, and she could hear him give the boys specific instructions about digging a hole in the backyard. Their old dog had passed on during the night, and they needed to bury the dog before the day grew too hot. She saw Marlin point the boys in the general direction where he wanted the hole to be dug. Then he hopped up on the wagon, loaded with extra vegetables from Hannah's garden to deliver to the roadside stand they shared with a neighbor down the road. She hoped he wouldn't get sidetracked talking to their neighbor. Unlike Hannah, Marlin was very outgoing and never ran out of things to talk about. Today, on this rainy day, she wanted him to get home quickly. She wasn't sure the boys could get much digging done without a man's help. And it was a sad task, too, Hannah thought, but it was part of life's cycle.

Hannah turned away from the window and tried rocking the baby to sleep for his morning nap. She was so tired. The baby, Joseph, had an ear infection and woke her frequently last night. She had been up a few times to check on their old dog, too, knowing it was his time. As she kissed the top of the baby's downy head, she felt washed with a wonderful love for this little bundle, fussy as he may be.

She could feel Joseph's little body finally relax and nod off when a door burst open downstairs and she heard the boys laughing loudly as they came into the kitchen. Joseph's eyes flew open when he heard his brothers' voices. Hannah sighed. She motioned to Ida, her nine-year-old, who was walking by her bedroom, to go down and tell the boys to be quieter. Ida went to deliver the message, then shouted up the stairs, "Mom! Come quick! You have to see this!"

Startled by Ida's shout, Joseph started to wail. Hannah wrapped a blanket around the baby and went downstairs to see what was going on. When she came into the kitchen, she could hardly believe her eyes. Her three sons were covered in mud, top to bottom. They looked at her, wide-eyed, waiting for a reaction. She couldn't even tell what color their shirts were. Woeful explanations spilled out of the boys. They hadn't gotten very far in the digging when they spotted a very nice mud hole nearby, so they fetched a stepladder and found themselves climbing up the ladder to jump in the mud hole. The squishy mud was so much fun that they tried it again and again. And again. Soon, the burial hole for the old dog was completely forgotten.

Wordlessly, Hannah handed baby Joseph to Ida and marched the boys into the bathtub. She spent the rest of the morning trying to clean both the boys and their clothes. Even after repeatedly rinsing their clothes, the water in the washer looked like melted chocolate.

As Hannah hung the shirts and pants to dry in the basement, she tried not to fan a smoldering anger toward Marlin. He should have been back hours ago. Where could he be? And why would he give the boys a chore, only to leave and let them carry on, unsupervised?

Hannah heard the sound of Marlin's horse, neighing as he trotted up the lane toward the barn. She waited, knowing Marlin would be awhile as he removed wagon traces and harness from the horse and made sure there was fresh hay and water in its stall. Besides, she wanted the boys to have an opportunity to tell him for themselves all that had transpired since he left.

Fifteen minutes later, she heard Marlin come into the kitchen and ask the boys, in his window-rattling voice, why that hole hadn't been dug. As the boys told him the whole story, Hannah slipped into the kitchen. She could tell Marlin was trying to look stern as he listened, but couldn't quite manage it. He avoided Hannah's eyes.

Unusually quiet, Marlin finished digging the burial hole for the dog all by himself. And he was particularly helpful with the children all afternoon. After supper, he took the family down to the barn to show them what had detained him that morning. There, in a crate, were two new puppies, spitting images of the family's old dog.

Later, Marlin admitted that he might have jumped in a mud puddle or two in his own time. "Anyone who knows Marlin wouldn't be surprised of this antic," Hannah said, shaking her head. She rolled her eyes and grinned. "Apples don't fall far from the tree."

ROAD MAP: GETTING THERE FROM HERE

Hannah's day didn't go as planned, but for her sons, the day unfolded in just the way they needed. Time to grieve and time to move on. Marlin knew his sons needed the pups—even more than they needed a burial. When your day doesn't go as planned, stop and take a breath. Look for the underlying cause for the day's derailment—it's quite possible that you are trying too hard to accomplish one thing and altogether missing the more important thing. The good is often the enemy of the best.

The Amish have a saying: "A sense of humor is like grease in the wheels of life." How does having a sense of humor help when faced with such a day as Hannah's? The next time you feel overwhelmed or exasperated by a turn of unexpected events, look (maybe dig?!) for the funny side of the situation.

In their own words . . .

A little boy went to his neighbor and asked, "Where's Henry?" "I'm not sure," replied Henry's mother. "If the ice is as thick as he thinks it is, then he's skating, and if the ice is as thin as I think it is, then he's swimming."

—Scribe from Mt. Hope, Ohio

I have learned when you send your husband to town with a grocery list, be careful how you write "oleo." He might come home with Oreos!

—Scribe from Anabel, Missouri

Workshop Raising

Very few burdens are heavy if everyone lifts.

Amish Proverb

John and Emma Troyer managed to save up enough money for a small workshop, separate from the barn, where John planned to start a custom cabinet building business. After four years working for a house builder—long days at distant job sites—he wanted to find a way to work at home and be available for his young family.

The Troyers bought all the necessary lumber and supplies, and then spread the word at church on Sunday that they would be hosting a workshop-raising frolic on Thursday. On Wednesday, the area was blanketed with about six inches of snow. Emma woke before dawn Thursday morning and saw bright stars in the sky. She hoped for a clear, sunny day, but as the family hurried along breakfast, clouds moved in and she was sure it would start snowing again. A circle of worrisome thoughts started to loop through her mind, again and again. Would their neighbors be able to come? Would the weather impede the building progress? John had already lined up his first customer. Would the workshop be ready?

By the time the sun was up, buggies were starting to roll into the lane. The women and children headed straight to the house while the men unhitched their horses from the buggy tracings. A couple of young boys took the horses out to a fenced pasture.

Sounds of hammers and saws soon filled the air. The men worked with minimal conversation, each intuitively knowing his task. In the warm kitchen, the women chattered all the while as they prepared the enormous noon meal. Children ran back and forth between job site and kitchen, delivering messages and "testing" food as the women prepared dishes. As often as she could, Emma paused to watch the beehive of activity. It filled her up, deep down, to see so many people working on their behalf.

The church wagon arrived by mid-morning, filled with benches. The man who brought it set up tables to provide enough seats for everyone for the meal.

At noon, the sun finally broke through, making for a gorgeous winter day. Emma directed the children to set out a row of bowls on a bench. She filled the bowls with hot water from a tea kettle. Clean towels were laid out beside the bowls. Then she sent her oldest daughter down to the work site to tell John that lunch was ready. The children watched as the men lined up and sloshed the water over their faces and arms, water dripping off their beards as they each reached for a towel to dry off.

Emma saw the wind start to kick up as a few women hung the damp towels on the clothesline to dry. A new worry—what would that mean for the crew working on the roof? She tried to quell her thoughts and turned her attention to the flow of women teeming in and out of the kitchen carrying trays of pickled beet eggs, quivering Jell-Os, sweet corn and applesauce, and stacks of fresh homemade bread. The men were seated at the tables, which held big platters of roast beef and bowls with cloud-like heaps of mashed potatoes and gravy. There was Emma's famous bacon-apple potato salad, made last night because it's always better the second day. And

27

peach cobbler for dessert, still bubbling hot from the oven. The minister, a neighbor who had come to help, offered a silent prayer. After the men ate and went back to work, the women and children filled their plates and sat down to eat and continue visiting. After the food disappeared, the women cleared away the mess, and the conversations continued in the kitchen over dishwashing.

By late afternoon, the shop was finished, complete with vinyl siding and a sleek metal roof. Someone had brought dinner for the Troyers, knowing they'd be exhausted. Emma stayed outside, waving and waving, until the last buggy rolled off down the lane. Today, she felt she had witnessed the most beautiful thing she had ever seen. It nearly made her weepy to be in the presence of such practical love.

Road Map: Getting There from Here

John and Emma Troyer's workshop raising is a perfect example of how the Amish culture influences younger generations. The entire community is constantly passing on skills, traditions, and attitudes. This is the strength of the Amish community, this sense of support and closeness. There are all kinds of ways for families—*as* families—to serve others: church ministries, short-term mission trips, local nonprofit organizations. An Oregon family raises puppies for Guide Dogs for the Blind. An Arkansas dad and son went to Haiti for a week to help rebuild after the earthquake. A mom in California celebrates her birthday each year by asking her family to join her for a workday at a nearby women's shelter. This year, find one way your family could serve someone in need.

When work is to be done, the Amish don't exclude children or keep them at home with a babysitter. Instead, the children are part of the work party, given age-appropriate tasks. At a barn raising, a man will start a nail in wood and let a boy pound it in. A girl will shadow her mother in the kitchen as she helps to prepare the noon meal. Children learn by example. The next time you're lending a hand to a friend or a neighbor, look for a way to include your child in the project. Start small, start slow. But start.

In their own words . . .

On Saturday, several of the men were cutting wood at James B's place and cleaning up his yard. He is a local man who has cancer, and he has several trees that someone trimmed but didn't clean up the mess. Everyone enjoyed working together, eating fresh cinnamon rolls, and drinking coffee and hot chocolate. Many hands made the work light and whoever needed wood got to take some home.

—Scribe from Mountain View, Arkansas

The birds bested me on my lone sweet cherry tree, and we only beat them to eleven pints of none-too-ripe cherries. I had my twenty-dollar plastic owl perched on a pole two feet above the highest limb at the very center of the tree. There he sat staring threateningly at the raiders as they gorged! I convinced my wife, Ruth, to stroll through the orchard for a look-see. As we neared the scene, a movement caught my eye and a wren lit on the pole supporting my owl. She gave her "I'm home" chirp, then flitted to the opening in the base of the owl, where she fed her hungry little ones nestled safely within. We are offering a pretested, multipurpose owl to any new owner at a very reduced price.

—Scribe from Minerva, Ohio

Family Vacations

A happy memory never wears out.

Amish Proverb

The Wengerd clan holds tight to certain traditions. Last August, the entire extended family made their annual trek to a favorite lake for a weekend camping trip—a sixteen-year tradition. "Some things that happen every year," said Marjorie Wengerd, mother of seven, "are the lively singing and discussions around the campfire, brightly lit by the hollow log set on end." Marjorie said that her brother, Jake, keeps his eye open all year for such logs. "This last summer, it took seven men wrestling a huge, hollow, six-foot log upright into the red-hot embers of the fire pit, creating a chimney fire that was something to behold." The circle of people around the fire increased, and the hour grew late as folks lingered and had second helpings of Marjorie's special homemade peach ice cream.

Marjorie said that most of their meals are cooked outside over the open fire and on the grill. "For breakfast, we did fried eggs, scrambled eggs, potatoes, sausage gravy, and side pork on the grill. For one of the suppers, we cooked a campfire stew over the fire. One evening, we made bacon-wrapped jalapeño peppers over the coals and grilled some barbecued chicken. For dessert, we brought homemade brownies and chocolate chip cookies."

When the Wengerds first arrived at the campsite on Friday evening, word was soon passed around that the lake contained algae that was toxic to fish and deemed unhealthy for humans. "What?!" Marjorie said. "We can't go swimming? On the hottest weekend of the summer? Impossible!" Later in the evening, camp staff informed the Wengerds that the pool at the neighboring 4-H camp was available if they wanted it. "Did we ever!" Marjorie said. "We ended up being thankful for the algae. We did not need to wonder what critters were swimming with us in those clear waters like we usually do in the murky lake water. We wonder if we could arrange for algae next year?!"

Each family took a turn at bringing and preparing a meal for everyone. "We even started a new tradition," Marjorie said. "For the last two summers, my niece and her new husband have treated everyone to fresh doughnuts fried in a pan over the fire for breakfast. We all stand around and eat them while the glaze is still dripping off. You don't get fresher than that!" Marjorie's elderly uncle, Philip, led devotions each morning.

On Saturday, the men and boys went off to find a non-algae-fied stream to fish. "They had fun fishing but went through a lot of bait," Marjorie said. "I think they enjoyed feeding the fish the bait more than catching them to keep."

That evening, after a full day of volleyball and a rigorous game of softball that ended with a tie of nine runs, they made kettle corn in a large black kettle. "This was another new tradition we started this year."

A close brush with some overly friendly skunks caused some anxious moments. "Those skunks chased a few ladies into cabins for the rest of the night," Marjorie said. "And by the next day, it was time to pack up and head home. It was so nice to get away from all the work at home, but when we walked into our house, it seemed extra big after staying in tiny tents and cabins a couple of nights."

Over the years, the Wengerd clan has grown through births and marriages. "Our number is now forty-two, but it seems there is never a year when everyone can be there. Still, it's always a blessing to reconnect and find out what is going on in everyone's life. We always thank God when we arrive back home safely after the reunion, with added blessings and oh so many good memories."

ROAD MAP: GETTING THERE FROM HERE

Sometimes, the simplest things in life are the very best. Children often have a better grasp of that concept than adults. The Wengerds' family gathering was about as simple as a vacation can get: tent camping, food cooked on an open fire, swimming in a lake (or a pool!). And the joy of being together. As you plan your next family trip, think about what you want your children to remember. What memory is going to stand out for them—the place? Or most likely, the people. Factor that thought into your trip—wherever it might be.

The Amish keep in close contact with their large extended families. Relationships are vitally important. Have you ever tried to create a family reunion? The benefits are numerous: they give a family context and a sense of belonging. Children learn "the family story"—the wonderful parts and the not-so-wonderful parts. Even the sometimes embarrassing stories can be a powerful way for your children to soak up words of warning, caution, or regret.

In their own words . . .

Another lovely day has dawned after a most spectacular sunset last evening. The whole western sky was a vibrant orange, more than I can ever remember seeing! We all stood outside awhile, marveling at the handiwork of God.

—Scribe from Sligo, Pennsylvania

here's a whole lot more things in life than hav-
ke, being around for your kids."

AP: GETTING THERE FROM HERE

keys to contentment in the Amish life is that they
through predetermined priorities: faith, family, and
When faced with a big decision, they weigh its impact
e. How will it affect their relationship with God? With
ing such a plumb line for decision making helps to keep
d other things, such as time commitments—in a proper
e. Money is only a tool, not a goal.

an interesting fact: the word *priority* didn't originally have
That was because you could have only one priority. Consider
mily's top priority. Does your use of time reflect that prior-
es your checkbook or latest credit card statement? Taking a
ok at where you spend your money reveals what you value.
has to go? What has to be added? This exercise—albeit a little
ful—is a tangible way to determine if your life actually reflects
t you believe to be your top priority.

In their own words . . .

We have the saying "Make do or do without." Two of my little
nieces learned to make do with what they had available when
they couldn't find the glue stick. They used Chapstick instead!
The little cards they made for daughter Karen had the pictures
securely fastened, so it works!

—Scribe from Harrodsburg, Kentucky

Adlai called me an old man when I turned seventy. Now he is
also seventy, and I heard he said he isn't all there anymore after
cutting off his first finger on his left hand, and also cutting into
his thumb last Saturday on his table saw. He had it fixed at a

---

My kidney is doing its annual thing in ridding itself of calcium
deposits—stones, in layman's terms. Men are, in spite of a cul-
tivated macho image, real wimps when it comes to pain. And
I am no exception. Last year Rhoda and I attended a family
reunion in Indiana during the time of my affliction. Which was
a mistake. I fear that those cousins not acquainted with the real
me came away thinking, "The guy's a real grouch."

—Scribe from Auburn, Kentucky

Too Much Money

Unless there is within us that which is above us, we shall soon yield to that which is about us.

Amish Proverb

For the last five years, Gil Hostetler has worked for a construction company that builds houses. He has plans, though, to buy a farm soon. "Me and my wife, we've been saving every penny so that I can get home and stay there." Gil and Salome have three children. "This job—it pays real well. But money isn't everything. It just isn't so good to have Dad gone all day long."

The houses that Gil's employer builds are custom built, many with a million-dollar-plus price tag. Gil shakes his head at such lavishness. "I see these folks wanting these big grand houses, strapping themselves to pay the mortgage. Both the mom and the dad have to work to make those big payments, and then the house is empty all day. Little kids get stuck in day care, or older kids come in to cold, empty houses. I've seen it with my own eyes. These kids come home from school, nobody's home. They end up

watching t'
get into
strong op
my thinking

Farming ha
As far back as
unwanted parce
a tie to the land t
like the Hebrews, th
it and pass it on to fu

But in the 1970s, as
settlements in Pennsylva
to escalate, the Amish fel
settlements—Colorado, Ma
necessity, to find sources of in
factories or construction jobs.
issue for the Amish. They strugg
their families, yet without losing
life—raising their children with bot
on a farm.

By contrast, Gil thinks the non-Amis
lating wealth and assets. "Folks just keep
Bigger houses. Newer cars. Bigger televisio
out with these big debts, and they forget wh
They could live with a whole lot less stress if
back and live a little simpler. I think everybody
off if they learned to be happy living with less.
house. Drive a car until it's broke down for good.
would sure be better off if Mom and Dad were hom
tention to them."

Too much money.

"Folks start losing their way when they got too much
Gil said. "Amish or English, we just don't need to make mor

be-all and end-all.
ing a ton of cash.

ROAD M

One of the
filter decision
community.
on family lif
others? Ha
money—a
perspecti
Here's
a plural.
your fa
ity? D
hard
Wha
pain
wh

Paducah hospital. They offered him a $10,000 helicopter ride to a city to sew the finger back on with no assurance that it would be successful. He probably didn't think a finger was worth that much as he didn't go for it.

—Scribe from Jamestown, Kentucky

Thursday is Thanksgiving Day. We sure have a lot to be thankful for. Many friends, food in the cellar, a warm house, and the Lord in control. What more do we need?

—Scribe from Mt. Hope, Ohio

Christmas Day

The dearest things of life are mostly near at hand.

Amish Proverb

On a farm, Christmas morning is like any other day. The cows must be milked. The animals must be fed and tended to. But when the chores are finally done, Christmas begins like in any other home. On the Stoltzfus farm, the five children gather in the kitchen, eager to see what their parents had prepared while they were doing their chores in the barn. These children aren't looking for a decorated Christmas tree because that's not what the Amish do. But in front of each child's place at the table rests a small pile of presents, covered with a pretty dish towel. This is how Amish families exchange gifts: in the spirit of the three wise men who brought gifts to the Christ child.

The gifts aren't ready for opening, not yet. First, the family sits down to a special breakfast tradition: sizzling bacon, savory egg casserole, hot muffins, and cold cereal.

After breakfast, sixteen-year-old Lydia and her two younger sisters help their mother with the dishes. "And then we sit at the kitchen table while my grandfather pulls out his well-worn Bible and reads the Christmas story to us," Lydia said. "He does it every

Christmas morning. It's the only day of the year that he would read to us, so we all sit quietly and listen carefully."

Finally, Lydia's parents say it's time to open the gifts. One Christmas in particular stands out for Lydia. "We pulled off the dish towel to find lots of homemade gifts! Some cookies, candy, and nuts, usually a new dress for me and my sisters that my mother had sewn. Each of my brothers opened a new shirt. And my oldest brother, Elam, was given a pocketknife—something he had been hoping for. My sister and I were given some stationery for our letter writing. And books! We all love to read and share our books with each other."

After the children had opened their gifts, read a chapter or two of their new books, and polished off the Christmas cookies, Lydia's father stood and stretched his back. "It's getting a little cold in here, don't you think?" he said. "Elam, why don't you add some wood to the fire?"

Elam went over to the woodbin, opened it up, and let out a loud whoop! There were five pairs of used ice skates, one for each child. "They didn't all fit perfectly," Lydia said, "so Mom found us plenty of extra socks."

That afternoon, the family bundled up and went to Blackbird Pond. "Daddy taught us how to skate," Lydia said. "Lots of other families were there too, so we had a skating party. We made snow cream and stayed until the sun started to set and we were too cold to continue. I'll never forget that afternoon."

Too soon, it was time for chores. Even on Christmas evening, the cows must be milked, the animals need to be fed. "As I went to bed that night," Lydia said, "listening to the hum of my parents' voices downstairs, I thought about the happy day we had together. I think that might have been the best Christmas we ever had."

ROAD MAP: GETTING THERE FROM HERE

What appeals to you about the Stoltzfus family's Christmas? Write down some hopes you have for your own Christmas celebration this year.

One mother said that she and her husband give their children three gifts: one that the child has hoped for, one to share with siblings, and one for fostering spiritual development, like a book or a journal. If you could choose only three gifts for your children, using that formula, what would they be?

The Amish have a saying: "The best things in life are not things." They know that happiness never comes from more stuff in our homes but from more life in our hearts (John 10:10). Does it ever seem as if Christmas is out of control? If so, what is controlling it? Others' expectations? A culture of unrelenting consumerism? Or you?

First things first in the Stoltzfus family: gifts are opened only after a traditional breakfast and a reading of the nativity story in the Bible. What could you change in your celebration schedule to reflect a focus on the true meaning of Christmas—Emmanuel, Christ is with us?

In their own words . . .

Is it fair that the blessings of caroling seem to benefit the givers more than the recipients? However that may be, caroling is always synonymous with Christmastime. The youth had their caroling on Wednesday evening, then again joined us as a church when we went caroling on Thursday evening. Beautiful evenings for both events, and hopefully the joyful spirit of Christmas was conveyed to the ones we sang for.

—Scribe from Limpytown, Ohio

Joy can be found in the simplest things—in a snowflake that falls from the sky, memories no money can buy, a visit, a kind word.

—Scribe from Newmanstown, Pennsylvania

Bill Coleman and a Quilt

Pray for a good harvest but continue to hoe.

Amish Proverb

For thirty years, Bill Coleman owned and operated a successful portrait studio in State College, Pennsylvania. "I was photographing the most beautiful coeds [from Penn State] in the world," he said.

Life was good.

But life got even better.

One day a friend offered to take Bill on a road trip that would take his life in a drastically different direction. They drove out to a remote, isolated Amish village. "I couldn't even spell *Amish*! I had no idea Amish even lived around here. I'd heard about the Amish in Lancaster, but that's a massive tourist trap. I learned more in one month there than I had in thirty years."

Bill was hooked. He found himself returning time and time again to that small and all-but-unknown Amish village where only ninety-some families lived. "It's hard to believe, at the age of fifty, that I took a completely different life turn. I looked to these people and their lifestyle, and I wanted to know more. I really wanted to be part of it. Innocence is total here."

He closed his portrait studio and devoted himself to photographing the Amish. That was thirty-three years ago. Now eighty-five, Bill continues to head out to that same village as often as he can. His work on the Amish is acclaimed and exhibited around the world.

What is his favorite subject? "Children, children, children!" Many, if not most, of Bill's photographs depict Amish children, unposed, doing what children do: skating, pulling sleds, walking through fields, caring for animals. "None of my work is posed, and I think that's apparent. You can see it's naturalistic."

Bill is very protective of the Amish village and doesn't reveal any details about its whereabouts. The children he once photographed are now grown-ups with children of their own. One of the things he plans for on a trip to the Amish village is to allow for the unexpected. His best photographs, he says, come from being open to seeing something with fresh eyes. Quite a change from a studio with complete control over lighting, shading, elements, and posing.

"I go out there two to three times a week, unless there's snow," Bill says. "Oh, heavy snow . . . I can't go out enough. It's different every day. It's exquisite. I think my best work is in the snow. The deep snow." There's an Amish cemetery where Bill spends time, for many reasons—the history that's buried there, the story of early pioneering families. "The average stone is only about a foot high. After a heavy snowfall, what you see are these undulating waves of snow."

Bill has a great respect for the Amish and their way of life. He said that the interactions he's had with these wonderful people, their values, and their way of living have quietly altered his own values and perspective on life—all for the better. "They don't need help. Over the years, I realized what I was missing." He hopes that his photography can teach others about a lifestyle that can be different.

"The Amish believe in their children and know that good habits start at an early age. They teach their young ones skills, socialization, virtues, and most importantly, the keystone to their culture—cooperation and friendship." Bill said that in all of the years he has visited the Amish, he's never heard an Amish parent raise their voice to a child. "Those kids jump up and do what they're told. But the parents have said that they teach them to obey by encouraging them to emulate their older siblings."

When Amish children come home from school, they are taught to farm and care for animals. An Amish father once asked him, rather pointedly though good-naturedly, "So, I suppose you let *your* kids come home from school and watch that television machine?"

He didn't offend Bill. Not at all. In fact, Bill gets a kick out of Amish humor. "They have a unique sense of humor. It took me awhile to latch on to it. But they do have a good sense of humor."

There is a beautiful photograph Bill took of three brilliantly colored Amish quilts hanging side by side on a winter clothesline. "There's a story behind that picture," Bill said. "The quilt on the far right—it's a beauty. I offered the woman who made the quilt one thousand dollars, which I thought was an outrageous sum at the time."

But the woman refused to sell it to him. "Now Bill," she said, "what would I have to leave my daughter?"

Not much later, Bill heard of a dealer who came through the area and managed to buy that same quilt from the woman for an excess of eleven thousand dollars. When Bill saw the woman, he chided her for selling the quilt. "What are you going to leave your daughter *now*?"

After a moment's hesitation, she said to Bill, "Well, I have other quilts." Then she rubbed her fingers together and a gleam came into her eye. "I'll leave them *money*."

Road Map: Getting There from Here

Bill Coleman has a great admiration for the family dynamics of the Amish. He said that he has observed the Amish instill virtues in their young at an early age, especially cooperation and friendship. Amish children are willing workers, reaching for tasks with enthusiasm—without complaining. They work together as a team, as parts of the same body—the family. The same is true for us—it takes all of us working together to keep our home running well.

Amish siblings are taught to respect each other; the younger ones obey the older ones. It's never too late to instill a sense of respect among siblings. You set the tone by not tolerating bullying or rivalry or teasing in unhealthy ways. One Pennsylvania mom insisted her children attend each other's sporting events or musical performances. She found it was a way to validate each child's unique abilities and to encourage her children to build each other up—part of being a team.

Bill said he never heard an Amish parent raise their voice to a child. And yet, the children obey! The next time you find yourself raising your voice in anger, hold off. Take a deep breath. Then say what needs to be said, minus the anger. You will be far more effective by maintaining self-control.

Bill had a successful career as an owner of a portrait studio. He gave it all up to pursue something he felt passionate about—something he felt called to. What does such a change indicate about Bill? What does it say to you about planning to use your senior years to fulfill God's purposes for you?

In their own words . . .

A mother said to her little girl, "Eat your spinach, dear, it will put color in your cheeks." Then the little girl said, "Who wants green cheeks?"

—Scribe from Hamilton, Indiana

Busy summertime sometimes makes late nights for the farmers, so they like to catch a snooze whenever they can. This one weary farmer was in the field raking hay one day last week, when a shower of sprinkles went through. He decided to just wait it out, out in the field, and lay down on the windrow for a snooze. He had just dozed off when a police car came across the field. Someone from the road had seen the horses, with the farmer lying on the ground. Thinking there had been an accident, they reported it to the police, who came to check it out. Next time, honey, sleep under a tree.

—Scribe from Farwell, Michigan

Mothers-in-Law

A happy home is more than a roof over your head, it's a foundation under your feet.

Amish Proverb

Martha and Leah Lapp don't resemble each other—Martha, slow and deliberate, is nearly six feet tall, and Leah, an energetic, plump little bumblebee of a woman, barely grazes the five-feet mark—but they seem more like mother and daughter than mother-in-law and daughter-in-law. They cook together, shop together, and chore together, all while sharing plenty of conversation. "Leah's always been so good to me," Martha said. "She's like a daughter and a friend, rolled into one."

When Leah married David, Martha's youngest son, the couple moved in with her for six months. They planned to build a new house on Martha's acreage as David took over daily management of the farm. When the economy soured, the young couple had to postpone building the house. Six months rolled into two years. "I didn't mind a bit!" Martha said. "I've been a widow for . . . forever . . . and this old house gets awful quiet."

Moving day finally arrived for the young couple. "Leah knew that I was going to be lonesome. The day before they were set to move in, she brought me a new puppy, a tiny one. When it was time for bed, the puppy was left in the living room to sleep, which it did not like. It cried and carried on, and even had tears. So Leah wrapped the puppy in a blanket and took it to bed with her. There, the puppy slept just like a baby."

The next day, as planned, Leah and David moved into their new home. As dusk arrived, Martha heard a knock on her door. "There they were! Leah said she was worried about that puppy not sleeping through the night, so they thought they should stay tonight just to make sure it slept through." That night, the puppy started whining again. Leah finally left a light on in the living room, and the puppy had a good night's sleep. "We figured it was just afraid of the dark." Leah and David ended up sleeping at the house for another few days, until Leah was confident that Martha wouldn't be woken in the night by an unhappy puppy.

The Amish tend to have healthy relationships among extended family. It could be that such large families foster a certain detachment, an ability to "let go."

Another reason may be that the culture supports and values marriage and family, so an in-law is a welcomed addition. Lena Miller of Kalona, Iowa, an Amish woman with seven married children, said that she views her sons-in-law and daughters-in-law as her own children. "I love them as if they were my own. I treat them like they're my own."

Proximity may play a role in creating healthy family relationships. Many, if not most, Amish families live in very close proximity to relatives. Often, they share the same walls. A *Grossdaadi Haus* is common among the Amish—it's a small attachment to a large house. It allows elderly parents to live independently but close to a younger family. Amish farmhouses tend to expand out on the sides, just like a family grows.

"You just don't hear of a lot of 'family feud' type situations among Amish," said Erik Wesner, author of *Success Made Simple*.[1] "I'm thinking of a Pennsylvania friend in the not uncommon situation of living on the same property as his parents. His wife is in constant contact with her in-laws. It basically becomes family. She would often want to travel to visit her own family, which was halfway across the settlement, about fifteen miles or so. Obviously home is always home, but I've never sensed any issues among them, and I lived with them for two months. I would have to say that there is probably some of the same dynamic as in the English world, but with proximity being an issue, I would think that any issues either get worked out, or . . ." Erik paused. "Well, I'd bet they tend to get worked out."

Road Map: Getting There from Here

Martha wasn't Leah's own mother—yet they had a loving bond. The Amish revere and value family life, including extended family and in-laws. Like any family, some members are easier to enjoy than others, but they would never dismiss or exclude someone. Everyone belongs. Everyone has a place at the table. Everyone is valued. If you truly believed that, how would it motivate you to work out problems or tensions?

God cares how we treat our parents. He expects us to pay attention to physical needs of elderly parents, as well as emotional needs. What is one way you show your parents that they are valued? This week, find a new way to honor your parents/in-laws. Plan a trip or get-together. Write a letter or email, send pictures of your kids, or call.

For fifty years, one woman traveled three hundred miles to visit her parents on their anniversary and birthdays. Her parents had never attended church—not once in their entire life. This woman prayed faithfully for her parents to know the Lord, all the while continuing to foster a loving relationship with them. When her father was in his nineties, he became a believer and joined the church. Her mother soon followed suit. If you're in a similar situation, take heart! Include your parents and in-laws in your daily prayers. Praying for your folks and in-laws helps fan your love for them and lifts them up to God.

In their own words . . .

Someone once explained the difference between in-laws and outlaws. The answer: outlaws are wanted!

—Scribe from Uniontown, Ohio

The person with a healthy attitude is too busy to worry during the daytime and too sleepy to worry at night.

—Scribe from Millersburg, Indiana

And then there was this grandpa who went to an auction. There were some other Amish men there that he knew from another community. Later, at a little ways off, he saw a white-haired fellow that looked so familiar but he wasn't sure who it was. Every time he looked at the guy, the fellow was also looking at him. "Does he know me?" he wondered. All at once he realized he was looking into a big mirror! He said he just turned around and walked away, and he felt sure the "other guy" did the same thing!

—Scribe from Chepota, Kansas

The Christmas Bird Count

The forest would be quiet if no birds sang except the best.

Amish Proverb

T he state of Ohio has important airspace. It's part of two
different flyways, Atlantic and Mississippi, which are travel
routes for bird migration. Think of it as a highway in the
sky with exits and overpasses and interchanges, minus the concrete
and the signs. And the traffic jams.

In the spring and the fall, thousands of birds travel over Ohio
on their journey from far north to far south, often stopping to rest
and refuel on the shores of Lake Erie. There's a three-mile patch
of land known as Magee Marsh, where birds will gather for one,
two, or three days before resuming the flight. A long boardwalk
was built into the marsh to accommodate the bird-watchers who
come to observe the birds. "Every May, Amish families will hire
vans and come to the marsh," said Cheryl Harner, an environmental
activist with a popular blog called *Weedpicker's Journal*.[2] "It's really
quite a sight. I often see Amish family groups with many children,
including very small children. They are never shouting or running.
They seem to be 'culturally quiet.' These Amish families have a great
reverence and respect for nature."

Breeding birds can be seen along the walk, Cheryl says, including great horned owls, Carolina wrens, tree swallows, and prothonotary warblers. "The birds let us come so close to them. They're tired from their long flight. They're not paying attention to humans." She smiled. "A 'bad' day on the boardwalk is still one of the best days a naturalist could have."

Cheryl is a devoted birder and often goes out to spot a rare bird on an Amish farm. "There seem to be two separate pastimes among the Amish—hunting as families, and bird-watching as families. Holmes County Amish are known for their bird-watching. They're serious birders." She says that a good chase for a rare bird often happens in Amish country. "Amish farms encourage bird population. If a bird lands in an Amish field, it will stay." Cheryl explains that the Amish use much less pesticide, if at all, than English farmers. "They have a healthier way of farming that allows for insects to survive, and that entices birds." One example, she says, is the kestrel, a small bird. "Kestrels are declining across America, but the numbers are rising in Ohio near the Amish farms."

While birding activities continue all year, it's the Christmas Bird Count season that involves the largest numbers of Amish birders, writes Bruce Glick in *American Birds*.[3] How did all of this get started? Local birders, according to Bruce, are quick to give credit to influential teachers who have helped students discover the beauty of nature and the wonder of birds—both Amish teachers in private schools and non-Amish teachers in public schools. The Christmas Count started in Holmes County in 1989 and quickly caught the imagination and attention of the Amish community. Bruce says that more than 80 percent of the Holmes County Christmas Bird Count participants are Amish birders. "One of the keys to success," Bruce writes, "is the encouragement of young birders. These youngsters can tag along, gradually learning the birds, and eventually becoming leaders themselves. On the most recent Millersburg Christmas Bird Count were 113 participants, of which thirty were eighteen or younger. Many of these young folks are amazingly good birders already, having spent years learning from older siblings, friends, and parents."

Amish birding is predominantly a male pursuit, Cheryl says, especially during the Audubon Christmas Bird Count. "It's only men and sons for the Christmas count. You wouldn't see Amish women out birding alone, but you'll often see families birding together on Sundays. Lots and lots of children!" During the Christmas Bird Count, Cheryl says, Amish teenage boys will bird by bike. "They set records of bird sightings. They take it very seriously and will only count the ones they see from their bicycles. If you offer them a ride, they'll say no."

Cheryl thinks the Amish are natural birders. "They have a better connection to the land than other people. They have a sense of stewardship. They're better observers. They listen to nature around them. They'll notice a different sound or a different look to a bird—even nondescript birds." Barn owls, for example, are very endangered in Ohio. "The Amish are the keepers of the barn owls. They need farm fields and pastured animals. Most of the barn owls in Ohio are on Amish farms."

She admires how the Amish model birding to their children. "The children have such a reverence and respect for nature. Even at play, they're not loud."

Recently, Cheryl visited her daughter in Florida. "I was flying home from Orlando, where countless English children show their lack of appreciation to their parents—even after hundreds of dollars were spent to entertain them at Disneyworld. Could you *imagine* their reaction if their parents told them the family vacation this year would be heading out to the woods to watch some birds?"

ROAD MAP: GETTING THERE FROM HERE

Cheryl said she often sees families birding together. Amish children grow up with a reverence and respect for nature. It's been modeled to them all of their lives! What is one outdoor activity your entire family enjoys? Make an effort to incorporate that pastime into your family life on a regular basis. One family has a Sunday picnic—rain or shine. If it rains, they picnic in their living room!

There are so many ways to encourage your children to be knowledgeable about nature—indoors and outdoors. Museums, aquariums, planetariums. Fishing, gardening, hiking, even a day at the beach. Make a list and get some dates on the calendar to expose your children to God's creation.

In their own words . . .

The joyful birds prolong the strain, their song with every spring renewed; the air we breathe, and falling rain, each softly whispers, God is good!

—Scribe from Wheatland, Missouri

In 2006, three young Amish birders had a friendly contest to see how many different species of birds they could find in one year. There was only one rule: all birds had to be found while hiking or biking away from home! During the next twelve months, bike tires were worn out and chores were done quickly. The boys spent so much time at the local Killbuck Marsh Wildlife Area that folks began to refer to them as "The Three Marshka- teers." They surprised everyone when all three totaled around 230 species, including a number of rarities. More importantly, they had a great time and learned a tremendous amount about the local avifauna. The boys are already talking about expanding the range of their biking trips in coming years.[4]

—Bruce Glick, "Christmas Bird Counts in Ohio's Amish Country"

Section Two

Great Expectations

A pulling horse cannot kick.

Amish Proverb

An elementary public school teacher taught her class about magnets. The next day, she gave them a quiz that included this question: "My name has six letters. The first one is *m*. I pick up things. What am I?" The teacher was stunned to see that almost half of the class had filled in the answer to that question with the word *mother*.

Amusing, yes, but with a sting of truth. We moms (dads, too) do too much for our children! This generation of parents has been more involved in their children's lives than any other before it, experts say[1]—but they also place few demands on their children. Whatever the reason—busyness (it's easier to do things ourselves) or overprotectiveness (our child needs our advocacy)—we just don't expect enough from our kids.

Short term, it *is* easier to do more for our kids. But long term? We end up extending our children's adolescence. "My son handed me a thank-you note to mail the other day," said Nancy, a mother of two. "He hadn't addressed it or stamped it. He doesn't know how! He had always just given me the written thank-you note, and I took care of mailing it. That was fine when he was ten . . . but he's twenty-one! Sometimes I think I've hobbled my kids with kindness."

By not asking enough of our children, we aren't helping them to grow up. In fact, they *aren't* growing up.

Among 2009 US college graduates, 80 percent moved back home with their parents after graduation. That's up from 77 percent in 2008, 73 percent in 2007, and 67 percent in 2006.[2] Today's young adults are going to school longer, job-hopping, and delaying marriage and children.[3] Sociologists debate what could be driving these changing attitudes. Some blame a dismal economy; others point out that many of these young adults are children of divorce and thus are in no hurry to marry. But one thing they all agree on: today's well-educated, media-savvy, and worldly kids just don't seem very mature—if maturity is defined by accepting responsibility for oneself and fulfilling expectations—compared with where their parents and grandparents were at the same point in their lives. In today's world, thirty is the new fifteen!

By contrast, no one could deny that Amish youth are well prepared for adulthood. A lifelong work ethic is well developed at a young age with household and farm chores. The Amish know that much of the on-the-job training for the workplace takes place at home as children participate in simple chores and tasks. They start children off with age-appropriate chores as young as three. As children grow, so do their responsibilities. Expectations are clearly set. Income earned by teens who work outside the home is handed over to a parent, most often for purchasing a future property or establishing a business. Most Amish young adults marry in their early twenties and start their families within a year or two. While Amish parents may help to initially finance a child's farm or business, the young couples quickly become independent and self-sufficient. And solvent. Marriage and parenthood, for Amish young adults, are valued goals, not burdens to be postponed. Adulthood doesn't come as a shock—they have been preparing for it all of their lives.

Taking the time to consistently train, follow through on expectations, correct, and encourage our children isn't always easy in the given moment, but such an investment of our time will return to bless our kids again and again. And the ultimate reward? Adulthood won't come as a shock.

August Pies

He is the happiest, be he peasant or king, who finds peace at home.

Amish Proverb

Every August, Fannie Yoder and Alice Byler set aside a day for baking pies, cookies, and bars to donate to the local fire station's annual consignment and bake sale. This last year, the day they chose was so warm that the two sisters decided to let the racks of baked goods cool on the floor of the enclosed porch of Fannie's house. The floor was tiled and on the shady side of the house, cooler than the steamy kitchen.

Their three children (aged two, three, and four) were happily playing with toys in the backyard while their mothers stirred and chopped and baked. Every now and then, Fannie or Alice would stick her head out the door to make sure the children were behaving. The last time she checked, Fannie did note that the children had taken off their socks and shoes and were running barefoot in the yard, but that didn't worry her. Satisfied that they were safe, having fun, and keeping out of trouble, she returned to her tasks.

The two sisters might have gotten a *bit* more preoccupied than they had anticipated with rolling out pastry dough and talking . . . more talking than rolling. Fannie took out the last blackberry pies from the oven and went straight to the porch. She gasped! The cooling pies had toddler-sized footprints in them, and tracks of toddler-sized berry footprints led to the back door. Every single pie had been stepped in. And Fannie's dog was licking clean an empty pie plate. Alice came up behind her with a hot tray of cookies and nearly dropped it when she saw the mess.

To add insult to injury, after rounding up the children and cleaning them off, they couldn't find any shoes and stockings. They spent the next hour hunting and finally found one shoe that had been chewed by Fannie's dog. Another shoe—a brand-new one—had been buried in the garden. It belonged to Fannie's two-year-old daughter, Mae. The two sisters never could find the socks, so they decided the dog ate them.

Next year, Fannie and Alice have decided they will hire a mother's helper for the day. "We had only ourselves to blame," Fannie said. "Last year, they were still babies and napped while we baked. We should have kept a closer eye on the children." As if on cue, a couple of loud woofs bellowed from the backyard. Fannie pinched her lips together in a line, as if she were trying not to laugh. "And a closer eye on that dog."

ROAD MAP: GETTING THERE FROM HERE

Fannie blamed herself for the disaster of that day. She expected too much of her children. And of herself! As she reflected on the day, she considered a way to do it better next time. Every parent makes mistakes—but the wise one is willing to learn from them.

Children and to-do lists often don't work well together. Today, don't write a to-do list. Instead, write a to-be list. Remind yourself of bigger, better goals: enjoying time as a family, making happy memories. One Amish mom in Missouri said it best: "Today was one of those days when I hardly got anything done that I had planned to when I got up this morning, but I have a sense that it wasn't wasted at all."

In their own words . . .

One little boy, Alex, went shopping with his mother to pick out a Father's Day card for his daddy. They found one that spoke when buttons were pushed. One button said, "Go ask Mother." In a very grown-up voice, Alex said, "That sounds just like Dad!"

—Scribe from Sugarcreek, Ohio

The sweet corn is in season and Micah, second son of Amos and Lora M., was helping his mother wash sweet corn they were going to cook for lunch. His mother left him alone a short time, and when she returned, the little boy had squirted a half bottle of dish soap on the corn in the sink. His mother had quite a time of washing it over and over till they could use it.

—Scribe from Belleville, Pennsylvania

Laundry Day

Teamwork divides the effort and multiplies the effect.

Amish Proverb

Wash day was the favorite day of the week for twins Lena and Wilma, now maiden ladies in their late fifties. On Monday mornings, after the breakfast dishes had been cleaned, the girls and their mother would collect the dirty laundry from the last week and take it down to the wash house, separate from the house. Then they would sort the laundry into piles. Lights with the lights, darks with the darks. To the girls' way of thinking, the piles soon resembled rainbow-colored corn shocks. Each pile would be put into five-gallon pails, old paint pails given to them from the hardware store, then they would fill the pails with water and let the clothes soak for a few hours.

Before lunch, the girls' mother would start boiling large kettles of water over a fire. Their father and five older brothers supplied plenty of wood so the fire would be well stoked. By the end of lunch, the water would be boiling. The girls' father helped to fill the wash tub with hot water before he went back to the fields for the afternoon. Their mother would first put the church clothes in the tub and add some soap. She took a plunger and agitated the soap, working the suds deep into the clothes for a few minutes. Then she got a long wooden stick—like a shepherd's crook—to lift the clothes out and into the rinse tub, filled with clean water. She would take one piece of clothing out of the rinse tub at a time and plunge it down into the water as deep as it could go. Then lift it up and let the water run off a little and then plunge it in again. She repeated the rinse cycle three times. Then the clothes were put through the wringer. Lena and Wilma helped feed the socks and smaller articles of clothing, but they weren't big enough to manage their father's or brothers' heavy, soggy work pants.

By the time they were done rinsing and wringing, the girls were usually soaked. "We didn't mind so much during the summer, but we would be shivering in the winter," said Lena. "The water sometimes froze up between loads in the winter."

The girls would fill a pail with freshly wrung clothes and head out to the pulley-style clothesline; it stretched right outside the back door down to the garden. Their mother often told them she didn't know how she managed before her girls came along. It was a long process that took most of the day, but soon all of the week's clothes were hung, luffing in the wind, clean and fresh. On very warm days, a batch of laundry might even be dry by the time they had finished with the last clothespin.

By late afternoon, nearly everything would be stiff and dry. The girls' mother would pull the clothes off the line. The twins stood with their arms stretched out—scarecrow style—to carry the load back to the kitchen, onto the large trestle table. Then they would run back outside to get another load. A mountain of stiff laundry grew and grew on the big table. When it had all been collected, they ironed, folded, and put away the laundry, singing a special hymn: "Wash me and I will be whiter than snow!"

Years later, in the 1980s, church members in the twins' district were permitted to get gas-powered washing machines that could agitate the clothes. One December evening, Lena and Wilma's father announced that he wanted to buy a washing machine for Christmas.

"Thank you, but no," their mother told their father in a tone of voice that said she meant it.

He was shocked. "But why? It would save you so much time! It would cut the job in half."

"As I wash those clothes," she said, "I use the time to pray for each one of my children. *That's* not time I want cut in half."

ROAD MAP: GETTING THERE FROM HERE

The Amish life of simplicity should never be confused with poverty or boredom. They are industrious and remarkably resourceful. Something as simple and mundane as washing clothes became a sweet memory for these two girls. They felt a sense of joy in their work, with an awareness of the peace and stability that routine can bring. And best of all, they knew that on laundry day, their mother was praying for them.

Think of a task in your life that feels mundane, even meaningless. How can this story's point—that even simple chores can have great meaning—adjust your perspective? One Maryland mom used trips to the grocery store to encourage her second grader to read. Together, they hunted for items on the grocery list and sounded out product names.

Prayer, for parents, is as necessary as breathing. Do you have a pattern of prayer established in your life, like the twins' mother did? One New Jersey father used his time on the morning commuter train to pray for his children, every day. A Wisconsin mom prayed as her children hopped on the school bus. Each day, she paused for a moment to pray as she watched it drive away. Look for an open moment in your day that can become a habit of prayer.

In their own words . . .

My sister Mary had just taken the towels out of the wash machine and felt something was still in the machine. She finally got it out and discovered she'd washed a mouse with the towels. She didn't bother rinsing the mouse nor rewashing the towels. With her two little ones, wash days can be hectic enough.

—Scribe from Dover, Delaware

To me, washing clothes is symbolic. It involves fire, water, and air.

—Amish mother of six from Gap, Pennsylvania

How to Make a Marriage Last

*Marriage may be made in heaven, but man is responsible for
the upkeep.*

Amish Proverb

R hoda and Tom Beiler have been married for forty-seven
years. "We understood the vows and thought we were very
much 'in love,'" Tom said. "But from the perspective of time
and experience, I now know that we didn't fully grasp the depth
of 'the tie that binds.'"

And that tie does indeed bind. It binds tight and holds firm. The
Amish have virtually a zero percent divorce rate.

By comparison, according to a recent study by the Barna Group,
the divorce figure among all born-again Christians (including evan-
gelicals) is 32 percent, which is statistically identical to the 33 percent figure among non-born-again adults. [4]

Amish wedding vows are viewed as a promise before God, taken
as seriously as a baptism vow. "A man and a woman know that this
commitment is for life," said Kathy King, an Old Order Amish wife
in New Holland, Pennsylvania, married to husband David for thirty

years. "They don't even question it. They know they have to make it through hard times as well as good times."

Kathy said that marriage partners don't expect perfection from each other. "We don't throw our faults into each other's faces. We live and let live."

Commitment is the key, said Dan Miller, an Old Order Amish bishop. "We make a commitment to each other. We work at it. We don't believe in trying to change your spouse. We're more accepting. And perhaps most importantly, we know that a happy marriage is pleasing to God." Dan and his wife have been married for more than forty-three years.

Since divorce is out of the question for the Amish, it might force couples to marry cautiously as well as to take a realistic look at how to fix problems, observed Erik Wesner, author of the blog *AmishAmerica*. "Mulling the divorce option in the back of the mind when things get tough in a relationship—I think that just sucks energy away from where it could be used constructively to strengthen a relationship. Not that that is necessarily the reaction of Amish couples to sit down and say 'hey, how can we fix this'— there are definitely communication issues like anywhere else—but the impact of the messages of Christian love that get repeated in Church and daily devotions and everywhere else in the culture cannot be overstated."

Erik also pointed out that the Amish lifestyle shapes an intimacy for spouses—both in close proximity and in relationship. "In contrast to the lunch-pail factory-work phenomenon and some 'on-the-road' businesses like construction, I'd say men who are farmers and home-business owners are still in large part in close and constant contact with their wives, which one would think would reduce issues that come from distance and alienation not uncommon in the more mobile modern society."[5]

The Amish are the first to say they are far from perfect. Some marriages turn sour. Sexual and physical abuse occurs. Church leaders have been known to abuse their power. In general, though, according to Dr. Donald B. Kraybill, a nationally recognized scholar on Anabaptist groups, the Amish way of life provides many sources of satisfaction for most of its members. Despite their imperfections, the Amish have developed a remarkably stable society.

A recent story in a newspaper sounded deliciously Amish. The reporter met with a ninety-two-year-old woman and her ninety-four-year-old husband. This elderly couple had been married for almost seventy years. "What's the secret to your marriage's longevity?" the reporter asked.

The couple looked at each other for a long moment. Then the wife spoke: "Eh, neither of us died."

ROAD MAP: GETTING THERE FROM HERE

The Amish believe that their marriage vows are a promise made to God, not to another person. Such a perspective certainly ratchets up the importance of that commitment! Amish children know that even if their parents have disagreements or difficult stretches, it doesn't threaten the security of the home. Those children are raised believing that marriage is permanent.

Today's children are growing up in a culture that dismisses—even mocks—the importance of marriage. Have you talked to your children about the seriousness of a wedding vow? Or about what an enduring marriage is based on? Share with them what God intended: marriage is designed to be a joyful, meaningful, fulfilling, and permanent relationship.

All marriages are bound to face trouble at some point. Chances are your marriage has already faced trouble, is facing trouble, or will face trouble in the future. Don't give up! Commit to pray daily for your marriage and wait expectantly for God's blessings when you do. Today is a new day.

In their own words . . .

When a man does dishes, it's called helping; when a woman does dishes, it's called life.

—Scribe from Mifflintown, Pennsylvania

The wife has an eye doctor appointment this week. She doesn't believe me when I tell her I get better looking every day, so she wants to get glasses to see if I'm right.

—Scribe from Carrollton, Ohio

A Teacher's Viewpoint

We pass on our convictions to our children by the things we tolerate.

Amish Proverb

The biggest reward to teaching is forming the bonds with the pupils," says William Byler, a teacher of twenty-four children in a one-room schoolhouse in Millersburg, Ohio. "I live in the same neighborhood as my pupils. I keep track of former pupils. We stay in contact."

William is a career teacher—a little unusual for the Amish. "Year after year after year," he says, "we're seeing more and more career teachers, rather than those who teach for a year or two." More men, too. Twenty-five years ago, mostly women went into teaching in Holmes County, Ohio. Today, William says, there are 38 male teachers out of 409 (200 schools). He explains that the school boards are offering better wages so that teachers, like William—who loves to teach—can make a living and support a family.

Today about thirty-five thousand Amish youth attend some thirteen hundred private schools that end with eighth grade. Most Amish children attended public schools before 1950. The Amish were comfortable with small rural schools that were controlled by local parents; in fact, some Amish fathers served as directors. As small public schools consolidated into large districts in the late 1940s and 1950s, Amish parents protested. They felt they were losing control over the education of their children. They also viewed formal study beyond the eighth grade as unnecessary for farming. In 1972, the United States Supreme Court, in a case known as *Wisconsin v. Yoder*, ruled that Amish children could end their formal schooling at the age of fourteen.

In some states, a few Amish children still attend rural public schools, but the vast majority go to one- or two-room schools operated by Amish parents. A local board of three to five fathers organizes the school, hires a teacher, approves the curriculum, oversees the budget, and supervises maintenance. Schools play an important role in passing on Amish values, developing lifelong friendships, limiting exposure to the outside world, and preserving Amish culture across the generations.

William feels the best part of an Amish education is that students are more involved with parents, more connected to the community. "I see it in my own children. They have time to do things. Active activities, outdoor activities." William says teaching is one of those jobs where the longer you're at it, the more you realize all you don't know. "I've learned more about nature from my pupils than they learn from me. Some of my pupils are avid birders. I'm a library, behind-the-desk kind of teacher. They're teaching me!"

Pupils in an Amish schoolhouse learn how to work together as one. "There's constant reinforcement of what they've learned," William says. "The younger ones hear the older ones' lesson, and the older ones get their learning reinforced by listening to the younger children." He likes to be imaginative in his teaching, to keep school from being dull. "We enjoy doing unique things, but not too often. Otherwise, it loses being special."

The focus of the Amish classroom accents cooperative activity, obedience, respect, diligence, kindness, and the natural world.

William is keenly aware of the differences between Amish and public education by the catalogs he receives from educational publications. "How in the world," he quips, "does a teacher use thirty-six 'You're #1!' stickers?"

ROAD MAP: GETTING THERE FROM HERE

William made an ironic comment: "What does a teacher do with thirty-six 'You're #1!' stickers?" The need to feel special—to be admired or envied—can become like an addiction. It doesn't satisfy for long. But feeling loved does. It's so important that we give our children assurance of God's unconditional love.

William said the best part of an Amish education is that students are more involved with parents. Parents are their child's first and best teacher. "More is caught than taught," is a common saying that points to the important role a parent plays. Remember *that* the next time you feel insignificant as a parent.

According to William, the Amish believe that educating the young is a community responsibility. That attitude should be—can be—ours as well! One Nevada family created a book drive and donated hundreds of books to the elementary school library. Another couple found out that their grandchildren's school principal was having surgery and organized a hugely successful donate-your-pennies drive to help the principal with medical bills. A California dad with now-grown children still donates to his children's high school athletic booster club—just out of appreciation. He attends games too. There are all kinds of ways—large and small—to encourage communities to get involved in education. This school year, look for one thing you can do to get involved. Everyone benefits when neighborhoods care about their children.

In their own words . . .

One mother asked her grade one son to name his favorite subject, now that he had a bit of experience in school life. The honest little boy, after giving it some thought, said, "Lunch!"

—Scribe from Seymour, Missouri

Public schools are in session again. Many mothers are so glad to have the children "out of their hair." We wish to keep them longer.

—Scribe from Salem, Kentucky

Snow Day!

No joy is complete unless it is shared.

Amish Proverb

In any school or church, one family always seems to stand out as having the "go-to" home. There's just something about that household that acts like a magnet to kids. They like to be there. It's hard to put your finger on what makes that one home stand out, because it isn't always true that it's the biggest home or the most lavish one or the most well equipped with entertaining technology. Usually, it has to do with the kind of mother in that home—generous, bighearted, forgiving. She cares about children. She notices them, and she's tolerant of a few extra shoes or wet mittens left by the door.

Sara Jane Bontrager is that kind of a mother. And the Bontrager farm is that kind of go-to home.

One Monday in January was a fun day for the children of rural Tennessee. "We woke up to a beautiful thick covering of snow," said Sara Jane, matriarch to a family of ten children. "We had been getting a lot of cold rain lately, and mud was everywhere. Nothing lately but gray and gloom. But when I woke up that morning, I felt my mood lift when I looked out the window. The sun shone brightly on the snow. It made everything look fresh and clean again. I just loved it. It's a reminder to me how God is in control of everything and he is the only one who can make everything look so pure and white."

After a special time of family devotions that followed breakfast, a knock came on the Bontragers' back door. It was Tommy, the neighbor boy, with a grin that stretched across his freckled face, coming to tell Sara Jane's family that school had been canceled.

The snow wasn't the problem, Tommy explained, it was the schoolteacher. She had visited her sister by bus and couldn't get back in time because the roads were closed.

Sara Jane's oldest, Menno, and Tommy hatched a plan. News traveled fast, and soon most of the schoolchildren had gathered at the Bontragers' farm to enjoy the snow together. The Bontragers' land has a good-sized hill on it, fondly dubbed the Big Monster, perfect for sledding on a winter's day.

"The snow equipment around here consists of anything from black plastic garbage bags to big pieces of cardboard to trash can lids to a long homemade metal toboggan. We aren't very choosy when it comes to a ride down the hill. Just so it slides. The sun shone so brightly on the snow that the kids were shedding coats and getting sunburned! My husband said he'd never heard of getting too warm while sledding. But then again, he's from Canada."

Sara Jane whipped up a large pot of chili, baked cornbread, and served a warm lunch to all of the children. "I think there were twenty children . . . no, twenty-two—I forget about those Mast twins, they're so quiet. Most of the kids scatter into the house like a flock of gabbling geese. Hungry, too."

Imagine "whipping up" enough food to serve to twenty-two hungry and cold children on a winter's day! But that's par for the course for Sara Jane. For the Amish. "I will say there were quite a few wet mittens and scarves by the door." She glanced at a large basket set by the back door. "A bunch of leftover ones too. I can't figure that out. You'd think somebody would notice they only had one mitten on." She lifted her palms in a helpless gesture. "Ah, children . . ."

On Tuesday, school resumed. "Much to the children's sorrow," Sara Jane said. "Yesterday was the kind of day that memories are made of, and yet nothing really important had happened at all."

ROAD MAP: GETTING THERE FROM HERE

Sara Jane Bontrager created an ambiance that made her home the "go-to" home for neighborhood children. She welcomed them, fed them (always a plus!), and allowed a margin of grace for the noise and chaos that accompanies children—leftover mittens and scarves by the door, a few extra lunch plates to wash. What are some of the benefits of having your home be a go-to place for your children's friends? Think of a few changes you can make to encourage it. One California mom provides hamburger and hot dog summer barbecues for her teenage son and his friends. Another family hosts their church's weekly youth group. A welcoming home doesn't have to be the biggest or the grandest. It just needs parents who welcome kids.

The Bontragers were able to stop, celebrate the snow day, enjoy it for what it was, and slip easily back into their regular routine the next day. They knew it was an unexpected, brief gift of time—not meant to last forever. The next time inclement weather provides you with a gift of time—enjoy it! And when it's over, get back into routine, refreshed from the respite.

In their own words . . .

We don't have very many hills around here, and a lot of sledding and skiing is done trailing with ropes behind horses and/or buggies. We found it a little humorous recently, when Chester and Katie S. were going somewhere one evening. Chester was skiing, and Katie and the baby were in the buggy. When Katie got there, she found she had "lost" her husband!

She backtracked and found him. It wasn't far, though. She knew he had been behind her when she turned the last corner.

—Scribe from Brown City, Michigan

A sign in front of a church near here had this snow request: "Would whoever is praying for snow please stop!"

—Scribe from Goshen, Indiana

Snowflakes are one of nature's most fragile things, but look what they can do when they stick together.

—Scribe from Grove City, Minnesota

Little Boys and Eggs

Half done is far from done.

Amish Proverb

One spring, Rebekah and Lloyd Schlabach decided to add a chicken and egg business to their family farm. Lloyd bought hundreds of fertilized eggs and set them up under warming lights. One morning, Lloyd took his three boys—Enos, age five, and twins Abel and Ray, age two—to check on the eggs. A few chicks had broken through their shells. Soon, another and another. "Right there as we stood watching," Lloyd said, sounding like a proud new father.

The Schlabachs' chicken enterprise was under way! And six months later, so was their egg business. It was Enos's job to collect eggs every morning and put them in the refrigerator in the house.

One morning, Lloyd had taken Enos to school, and Rebekah was busy upstairs changing sheets on the beds. "Enos must have been in a hurry, because he had left the basket of eggs on the kitchen table." Abel and Ray spied the eggs. "Their little eyes were tempted!" Rebekah said. "Off they went to the playroom with the basket of eggs. They used the toy box for target practice, throwing eggs at it like it had a giant red bull's-eye on it. What a mess! The eggs splattered all over the toys, floor, walls." Rebekah felt like crying. Her morning chores had just been rearranged.

"Lloyd and I had a long talk with the boys about taking that extra step to make sure a job is finished well. Enos felt badly about leaving the eggs out, I felt bad for not minding the twins." She paused and lifted her face to the ceiling. "I'm not sure the twins felt so bad. They had too much fun."

Rebekah felt satisfied that the lesson had been learned about not taking the egg business trivially. But later that week, Enos came running inside the house. "Mom, I found two more eggs!"

From across the room, Enos opened up his palms to show his mother the eggs, then he tossed them right at her.

"I was horrified! Until it turned out to be plastic eggs someone had brought to school. Enos laughed so hard at his own trick that he got all of us laughing, even the twins." Rebekah sighed. "Motherhood has its ups and downs." She smiled. "More ups than downs, thank heaven."

ROAD MAP: GETTING THERE FROM HERE

Lloyd grew up on a farm. He had been around chickens all of his life, yet when those chicks broke out of their shells, he stopped in awe at the sight of birth. Even the birth of a chicken! His example reminds us to never become blasé about the wonder and awe of God's creation. Every single day provides opportunities to admire God's handiwork.

Family businesses are the backbone of Amish livelihood. You might be astounded at the variety of Amish entrepreneurial industries: quilt shops, roadside vegetable and fruit stands, harness shops. One Amish father taught himself and his sons all about electricity. Now they hire out as electricians! What kind of a business could your family create? Something as small as a summer lemonade stand teaches basic business skills. Who knows? It could be the start of an enterprise.

In their own words . . .

We mothers were happy to hear a message for our work and calling on Mother's Day. When sons are grown and leave home, we mothers wince at the thoughts of the severed apron strings, happy as we are for their new home or vocation. But then on messages to mothers we will usually see the shimmer of tears at remembrances of godly moms from even the most battle-weary warriors. The influence and impressions are never forgotten.

—Scribe from Romulus, New York

The boys ended up being farmers this week. Our neighbor, Steve F., sprained his ankle real bad on Sunday so he wasn't getting around very well. We offered our boys' help to do the milking. They had to get up shortly after 5:00 in the morning, bike up, do the milking, and then walk through the chicken house yet. The first few times it was fun, but by the end of the week they were dragging at the tail. All in all, it was a good experience for them.

—Scribe from Millersburg, Ohio

The Do-Over Boys

The more a child is valued, the better his values will be.

Amish Proverb

The kitchen timer on the teacher's large wooden desk in the center of the classroom is ticking away. It's 9:25 on a warm, sunny April morning. Twenty-seven Amish children are quietly cleaning the tops of their desks, putting their books inside. A few are whipping off their socks and shoes, trying to beat the buzzer.

The buzzer finally goes off. Recess! The children waste no time hurrying to the storage room to get lunch snacks out of their small igloo containers, plus a ball, bat, and a few gloves. All but two boys with mournful looks on their faces. Their names are written on the chalkboard under the label "Do Over." These two are stuck inside for recess.

Anna, the nineteen-year-old schoolteacher, explains that these two boys often put off their work, and it is time they learn to correct the habit of procrastination. "They're smart boys," Anna whispers. She points to the tall one. "He's the smartest one in the class. But he can be lazy." Anna is wearing a traditional Amish collarless dress, lavender colored, with a cape covering her shoulders, and black socks. No shoes!

Outside, a few of the young boys head to the far end of the field to toss a ball back and forth, but most of the children play a game of softball. A batter hits balls to the fielders, and positions are rotated as a batter gets to base. The outfielders back way up when Ruthie, a redheaded, athletic teenager, takes a turn at bat. And they come way in—way, way in—when Katie, a tiny first grader in a dusty plum dress, goes to bat. After Anna has made sure the Do-Over Boys are hard at work, she puts on her sneakers and heads outside to take a turn as pitcher. The excitement level on the field rises a few notches, especially when Anna is up to bat, but no one eggs on the batters or the fielders. There are no arguments or disputes over strikes or foul balls, only encouraging calls.

The fifteen-minute recess ends when Anna rings the school bell. A few students stop to get a drink of water from the old-fashioned pump, but their entry into the schoolhouse is orderly and prompt, and quiet soon fills the room. Anna gives a nod and a student leads the children, single file, to the back of the room to grab a hymnbook. One by one, they march up to the front of the class and form three rows, the tallest children in the back.

They sing three hymns. Anna allows the Do-Over Boys to pick the hymns. They look considerably happier now. The first hymn is the recognizable "Give Me Roses While I Live." Anna's clear tenor leads the children through the songs without benefit of a piano. The second song, "Rose of Sharon," is sung in four-part harmony, a cappella. The third song, "Rose of Calvary," is also sung in four-part harmony. The children sing in English. Although Amish children speak Pennsylvania Dutch in their homes, they learn English in school. Even on the playground, the children speak English.

This is Anna's first year as a teacher. She replaced another teacher who had taught for three years but had trouble getting obedience out of the scholars. "The girls were especially difficult," Anna says. "Girls can be hard." The classroom has fourteen girls, mostly older, though only one wears a prayer cap. Girls don't wear caps until they are in eighth grade, Anna says. She is very soft-spoken with the children, and they mind her well. She says it took months of consistency and clear expectations before the classroom operated as efficiently and cooperatively as it does now. "All fall, I could only say I had a job," she says. "Now, I can say I love it. And I do. I really do."

Anna glances in the direction of the Do-Over Boys, whose heads are bowed over their desk, working away on their arithmetic. She erases their names off the chalkboard and smiles.

Road Map: Getting There from Here

"Discipline," one Amish mother said, "is for the good of the child. We never discipline out of anger, but to communicate appropriate behavior." What made the concept of "Do Overs" such an effective form of discipline for those boys?

When the boys had caught up with their work, the discipline was over. Lesson learned. Anna even let the Do-Over Boys choose the hymns to sing. They were gently restored, welcomed back into the fold. What a wise example for us—this is how God treats us after repentance! God's discipline is always kind (Heb. 12:5–6).

Does it surprise you that Anna, at the tender age of nineteen, had such a clear vision of how she wanted her classroom to operate? It wasn't easy, though. It took months to shape the atmosphere in her schoolhouse. Remember Anna's steadfast perseverance the next time you are faced with a similar challenge. She had a vision, made a plan, and stuck with it, patient and determined to see it through.

In their own words . . .

One young boy, after hearing a very inspiring sermon from a visiting minister, innocently remarked, "I almost couldn't help but listen!"

—Scribe from Sligo, Pennsylvania

Sunny View School had pet day last Tuesday. Rabbits, dogs, a rooster, and a pony found their way to school. And if you want to invite the pony into the schoolhouse for a visit, make sure he is potty trained. This one little boy had a cleanup job to do, amid the grins of classmates! At least they all had some great pony rides at recess!

—Scribe from Clare, Michigan

The Girdle

Keep your words soft and sweet just in case you have to eat them.

Amish Proverb

At fifteen, Elsie Hershberger was a little heavier around the hips than she wanted to be. On the farm in Indiana where she grew up with three siblings, the kitchen was always filled with freshly made baked goods. Her mother was a fine cook, and Elsie had a sweet tooth. She didn't feel unattractive. Elsie had plenty of young Amish fellows buzzing around her. But lately, the extra padding around her middle bothered her.

So Elsie decided she needed a girdle.

Her mother, an Amish woman who had little patience for such nonsense, refused to buy her daughter a girdle. But Elsie couldn't stop thinking about that girdle. She kept at her mother, trying to wear her down. Her mother would not budge. To her way of thinking, a girdle was not necessary, it was not healthy, and it was not the Amish way. But to Elsie's way of thinking, a girdle was very necessary.

One afternoon, after yet another fruitless discussion with her mother about getting a girdle, Elsie marched to the barn. "My mother was small and petite, she never yelled at us children, but we always knew she meant what she said." Elsie was beside herself in teenage anguish, sobbing, and decided to seek out her father. "My father was more of a free spirit than my mother. He was always very 'fuzzy' about things." Surely, he would understand her despair. When she found him, she poured out the story to him. "Mom won't let me get a girdle!"

Surprised and more than a little embarrassed with the discussion of ladies' unmentionables with his eldest daughter, her father said to her, "Well, if it's that important, then, go get yourself a girdle."

So Elsie went into town, straight to the five-and-dime, to spend her precious few dollars on a brand new girdle. Later, when she returned home, she went to her room to try it on. An hour later—or was it only moments?—Elsie decided she had had enough of feeling like she was a sardine squeezed into a can. She took off that hideous contraption and tucked it in the back of a drawer.

Why on earth, Elsie wondered, had she ever wanted a girdle?

ROAD MAP: GETTING THERE FROM HERE

Elsie's father showed great wisdom. He gave her the room to practice decision making. He let her experience spending consequences for herself. His parenting wisdom could be applied to anything our children desperately want. Elsie's father didn't buy the girdle for her, and he didn't return it when it ended up being a disappointing purchase. Elsie learned a lesson she never forgot—that things don't always live up to your expectations.

When eight-year-old Alexandra badgered her mother for pierced ears, her mother told her she had to wait one year from that very day—to be sure she wasn't making an impulsive decision. One year later, Kim took Alexandra to get her ears pierced. As Alexandra saw the instrument tray, including needles, she changed her mind. Within reason, we need to give our children reality checks about money and purchases and desires.

In their own words . . .

While out in the pumpkin field, Jake A. and Lovina S.'s cow took a bigger bite than what she could chew. She had a whole pumpkin wedged in her mouth. She was taken up to the barn, and Jake managed to make a hole in the pumpkin with a hammer and pull it out.

—Scribe from Montgomery, Michigan

Whdim! Whdim! Hummingbirds zip past the feeder hanging close to our dining room window and zoom into a nearby tree. Although there are four flower-shaped feeders and four birds, they never have a relaxed meal together. One self-appointed boss is so busy making sure the others don't get more than their share of the nectar, he can't even enjoy drinking it himself. Recently a bee has moved in, and he's even bossier than the boss. When he straddles a flower and takes up the guard, all the hummingbirds are out of luck. I wonder if God views us as being just that foolish when we get our hackles up to protect "our interests."

—Scribe from Pantego, North Carolina

Amish in the City

You can tell when you're on the right track. It's usually uphill.

Amish Proverb

I n the summer of 2004, a reality television show called *Amish
in the City* was aired on CBS. It featured five Amish young
adults—three men and two women—put them in a house in
Los Angeles with six similarly aged non-Amish urbanites, and let
the cameras roll.

Emmy-winning producer Jon Kroll, the creator and producer
of the show, came up with the idea for the show after learning
about Amish *Rumspringa*—a Penn Dutch word that means "running around." (Rumspringa is a misunderstood concept among
the non-Amish. When an Amish youth turns sixteen, he starts to
attend youth gatherings. It is popularly thought to be a time when
Amish youth sample the temptations of the world before choosing
to become baptized.) A child of the seventies, Kroll grew up on a
commune in a remote part of Northern California—no electricity,
no indoor plumbing, no pop culture. He could relate to the isola-
tion of Amish teens and was intrigued by the concept of letting

young people experience the world before deciding whether or not to join the church.

The concept for the show was snatched up in two days. Then Kroll went to work to find the cast. "It was unlike the casting process for any show I've ever been a part of," Kroll said. "We put together five two-person teams and sent them to different towns near Amish communities, where they lived for two months. They were producers, not traditional casting directors, and in many cases we used them on the series, to take best advantage of the knowledge and experience they gained by spending so much time around Amish people."

Naturally, Kroll said, most of the Amish youth who expressed interest in doing the show were considering leaving the church. The five Amish teens who were ultimately cast were on the fence about remaining Amish—not committed to leave, not committed to stay. "We turned down those who said they were certain to leave. Our approach was very straightforward—we told them that if they were considering rejecting the outside world, wouldn't it be better to see what the outside world was like so they would know what they were rejecting? This question was the driving force for us in undertaking the show—we felt that the Amish way of life was attractive and resonated enough that it could stand up to a comparison to big-city life, but we did not see evidence that many young Amish people were able to experience city life in any meaningful way prior to making the choice. We wanted to give them that experience."

What Kroll didn't anticipate was the controversy that erupted when the show was announced. Outcry rippled as far as the House of Representatives in Washington, DC. A petition to cancel the show was spearheaded by Congressman Joseph Pitts (R-Pennsylvania) and signed by fifty-one other congresspeople. Kroll was surprised by the vehemence of the opposition and the assumptions that he was exploiting or disrespecting the Amish. Such a thought had never occurred to him. He had always intended to be respectful toward the Amish.

The show was an immediate summer hit. Ratings started high and stayed high; reviews were very favorable. Curiously, the show did not reflect badly on the Amish. Just the opposite. The Amish kids seemed tolerant of the urban kids, were kind to each other, and were grateful—so very grateful. If anyone looked bad, it wasn't the Amish. It was the English roommates. They were shockingly rude, cynical and snobbish, insensitive, and often just plain stupid.

Creating a cast of contrasts was part of the plan. Like the Amish, the six city kids were at a crossroads in their own lives. Each was an extreme of its stereotype—a devout vegan provided a stark comparison to one Amish girl raised on a dairy farm, for one example. The one thing these city kids all had in common was a desperate need to be special and a love for the spotlight.

"Since I was raised without television, telephone, and electricity as well," Kroll said, "I know that growing up without those influences changes you. It makes you connect differently with other people and your surroundings. I think this was reflected in the show by how appreciative the Amish young people were of each other, their city roommates, and the producers for that matter. I also think they got a lot more out of the experiences they had while living in Los Angeles . . . especially in light of their city counterparts taking so much for granted."

Six years later, Kroll still feels he's never been prouder of a show he's produced. "This was the first unscripted show to directly deal with issues of faith and family in a meaningful way."

What Kroll hadn't expected was to be influenced by the Amish kids. "Everyone who worked on *Amish in the City* and everyone who was in the show was profoundly changed by the experience. And that's never happened on any show I've ever done, before or since. . . . Their most compelling lesson to us was to appreciate the people and things we have in our lives and not to take them for granted."

ROAD MAP: GETTING THERE FROM HERE

Be honest. Did you start this story with a fixed opinion about the TV show *Amish in the City*? Did your feelings change after you read the story and learned about producer Jon Kroll's upbringing? How did they change after you read that he felt changed by the experience of working with the Amish? It's something we all should aspire to: to inspire others through authentic faith.

Rumspringa varies greatly, from church to church, from family to family. The concept of Rumspringa is successful (if you consider the high retention rate of Amish teens—85 to 90 percent join the church) because parents trust that what they've put into their children is deeply embedded. They can give their young adults some breathing room for experience because they've done their job well. When your teens start to spread their wings, ask yourself—have I done the best I can to prepare them for a life of faith? If the answer is yes, trust that those lessons will remain present in their lives. Trust that God is faithful, even when we (and our children!) are not (2 Tim. 2:13).

In their own words . . .

I have to write about the split in our church. That has been interesting. It happened on Sunday morning a few weeks ago and involved some very solid brethren. Naturally, there were signs a long time before it happened, but everybody was busy and must not have communicated sufficiently. So, when we turned around and knelt for prayer and there was a loud report from somewhere toward the back of the church, we didn't know what had happened. What happened was that the split in the bench seat had become a break, and when the brethren sank to their knees, half of the bench seat descended with them. To their credit, after prayer they preserved their sobriety and perched on the remaining half of the seat until the service was over. Lateral rifts have appeared in other bench seats, including the one on which I sit. Sure hope it gets fixed.

—Scribe from Farmington, New Mexico

Then there was this guy who was visiting and looked for a place to sit. He found what looked like a high stool of sorts and sat on it. One of the little children informed Mom that one of those men was sitting on the bread dough. Since bread dough needs to be warm to rise, I assume it turned out all right.

—Scribe from Loyal, Wisconsin

Read, Read, Read

Peace is seeing a sunset and knowing whom to thank.

Amish Proverb

As a young boy growing up in Holmes County, Ohio, in the 1950s and '60s, David Kline was painfully aware of his speech impediment. "I stuttered. It was so bad I thought I'd never marry." So David compensated by turning to reading. "I loved words. My stutter turned me on to reading. I read everything I could get my hands on. My parents were readers and encouraged us to read. I read a lot of nonfiction—Henry David Thoreau and Hal Borland. Even *Huckleberry Finn* by Mark Twain. That was the most original American novel. It helped that my parents were readers. My whole family read. Remember, we had no television."

David attended Elm Grove, a one-room public school with a Mennonite schoolteacher, the legendary Clarence F. Zuercher. In a happy coincidence, Mr. Zuercher had taught David's father when he was a boy. If a teacher was considered good, David said, he had the run of the school. And Clarence Zuercher was good.

This teacher opened David's eyes to the natural world. He immersed his scholars in flora and fauna, birds and insects. Nothing escaped his keen sense of observation. "Mr. Zuercher influenced so many in a positive way," David said, lighting up at the mention of his beloved teacher. "He was such a free thinker. He taught us to love God's creation. He taught us to observe and identify all aspects of nature: stars, trees, flowers, leaves, bark, soil, insects."

In the springtime, Clarence Zuercher would dismiss school early so he could take the boys fishing. "He even took us to local streams to fish. We used fish worms and cane poles." David said everyone knew they were in the presence of a master fisherman who understood fish as well as he did the shenanigans of schoolboys.

When the time came for the dreaded eighth grade state exam in the spring, Mr. Zuercher shooed the eighth grade class out into his 1952 Ford to study and catch up in reading for the exam. (Unlike the Old Order Amish, most Mennonites do drive cars and have electricity in their homes.) "He never let the classroom interfere with our education," David recalls. "I don't remember ever getting through a textbook before the school year ended in late May. As the time was getting close, he told us to read, read, read. He'd send us out in the car so we wouldn't be distracted by the other classmates and the classroom dog. Of course, he sent the keys along so that we could listen to the radio." There were only two boys and one girl in the eighth grade. The girl, David said, took the front seat of the car. "Naturally, we endured the country music she preferred. We thought it was silly that every mournful singer either lost his dog or his car or his girlfriend."

David remembered a time when a student was gazing out of a window of the schoolhouse and spotted a Goodyear blimp. The students were sent outside to watch the huge airship crawl through the sky as slowly as a snail crossing a road. Mr. Zuercher praised the daydreaming student for his sharp eyes.

David's self-conscious stutter turned him to writing. He became fascinated by the words that he could write or read but never utter in front of people. "Those twenty-six letters of the alphabet intrigued me. So did the dictionary. There were infinite ways to arrange words to describe the boundless beauty and mystery beyond the doorstep."

What happened to David's childhood prediction that he would never marry? Didn't happen. He married his sweetheart, Elsie, after serving as a conscientious objector during the Vietnam War. They have five children. And what about his stutter? "I grew out of it," he said. "I learned to laugh. Still have a fear I'll freeze up. But God let me have that stutter for a reason. Perhaps because it turned me to writing."

Years later, David wrote two naturalist books, *Great Possessions* and *Scratching the Woodchuck*. He and Elsie are the owners and editors of *Farming* magazine, a quarterly journal committed to farming in harmony with nature. After all, it was the way he was taught by Clarence Zuercher.

ROAD MAP: GETTING THERE FROM HERE

Born in 1896, Clarence Zuercher lived a long and productive life before he passed away in 1974. David was given access to his personal diaries—a gift of great value. Who was a significant adult in your childhood? How did he or she influence you?

David Kline said, "While most children today are on computers or watching TV, we were playing games, puzzles, reading books, or out enjoying nature." Most American kids are quite competent with technology and far less familiar with nature. How aware are your children of the natural world? One husband built his wife owl boxes for Christmas and attached them to trees in the backyard. Now the entire family listens for the hoot of the owls on warm spring nights. Consider one step you can take to bring a greater awareness of nature into your family's life.

Most people, when observing nature or wildlife, feel a sense of calm and peace. It takes intention, though, to slow down and notice the world around you. When those quiet moments come, savor them. One Ohio Amish farmer said, "When we appreciate

God's handiwork, it gets our mind off earthly things and more on heavenly things."

Did it surprise you to read that Clarence Zuercher praised the daydreaming student for his sharp eyes? The point he made wasn't to applaud daydreaming; it was to pay attention to the extraordinary! Take a lesson from Mr. Zuercher and point out wondrous moments to your children: a brilliant rainbow, a night sky filled with diamonds, a Goodyear blimp sailing in the sky.

In their own words...

The boys at Ash Grove School wanted to catch rabbits in the worst way when we had our snow, so the teacher said, "Okay, we'll try it." They made a circle around a brush pile, and a few got on it and scared three rabbits out, with one running between the teacher's feet—and she caught it! The children then had a lesson in skinning and cleaning a rabbit. I expect the rabbit learned what the children already knew: you won't slip anything by the teacher.

—Scribe from Clark, Missouri

Teaching can be quite interesting at times. The teacher was telling the story of the ravens feeding Elijah and trying to make the point of God supplying our needs. In an effort to get the children involved in the lesson, she asked them what are some things that they need. Little Katie Yoder raised her hand and said, "We need a dishwasher!" Hiding a grin, the teacher explained the difference between "needs" and "wants."

—Scribe from Walnut Creek, Ohio

Interlude

A Year in an Amish Family

No winter lasts forever. No spring skips its turn.

Amish Proverb

A few years ago, I met the Simon Yoders while doing research for a book. The following story is what I've learned and observed about them from visits with the family and through letters I've exchanged with Edna Yoder.

Life and work on the Yoders' Ohio farm revolve around seasonal rhythms. The four seasons order the flow of daily work that involves every member of the family—with help from the oldest (Simon's dad, Ivan, age seventy-seven) and the youngest (Simon's daughter, Rose, age six). Amish families garden together. Simon and his wife, Edna, prepare and plant the plot together. During summer harvest, the entire family—nine children (five boys and four girls) plus widower Ivan—pitch in to get the field crops in.

Working together to benefit the family has been the backbone of Amish tradition. Day by day, month by month, the layers of hours nurture the family's sense of belonging. The passing of time, governed by a yearly cycle, spins along, sweet and rich with meaning.

On December 31, Simon prays this prayer just as his father and grandfather had prayed it: "Lord, all this year you have tenderly watched over my friends, my loved ones, and me. You have truly blessed us. Now, may we live each day of the New Year protected and surrounded by your love."

In late winter, Simon gets restless for spring to arrive. "Farmers have had enough of their coffee breaks, though winter is a good time for such things like that if we can get through the snow! The snow and ice have melted somewhat; we hear drip, drip, drip from the icicles formed on the edges of buildings. But there are still high snow piles around. Some of these piles have tunnels dug through them made by the children, and others [piles] were used to play King on the Mountain at recess time."

Spring is a time of reawakening. Most of the Yoders' field work happens between early March and late October. The intentionally limited size of Amish farms means there is usually something to do without being overwhelmed by work.

Horses become conditioned for the growing season through the leisurely plowing of sod as Simon prepares the fields for spring planting. "The fields are starting to have a hue of green," Edna writes in late March. "Even though we like white winter months, there is something special about new life bursting from the ground and trees. Oh, the wisdom of God in the changing seasons!"

April is for plowing cornstalks and sowing oats, and preparing Edna's sizeable kitchen garden for summer's bounty.

In May, past the point of freezing, Simon and his two oldest boys plant corn. Cows and horses are turned out to pasture. Crops are being cut for hay baling. "Suddenly everyone is busy," Edna writes. She revels in returning purple martins—nature's efficient bug control.

"When we were still young and going to school, it seemed like the days just dragged by," Simon adds. "Especially toward the last part of the school term when the weather got nice and warm and the birds started coming back and the leaves started coming out. Now, the days seem to simply fly by."

By the end of the month, school is over for the Yoder children, and shoes are abandoned for bare feet. "Fireflies are blinking away at night, letting us know the busy season of summer is fast approaching," Edna writes.

With hay making in June comes a sweet smell of strawberries in the air. The birds are singing, with their young ones flying from the nests. June means cosmos and snapdragons blooming, butterflies and bumblebees hovering. "Ripe strawberries—the sweetest things you ever tasted—bring treats from Edna's kitchen: shortcakes, pies, and jams," Simon says.

Summer is settling in. "It's hard to believe that we've now already passed the longest day of the year," Ivan says, "and it begins to wind down toward shorter days." How quickly a coming season treads on the heels of the departing one.

Life and work on the Yoder farm peaks in July with threshing, second-cutting hay, early apples, honey from Ivan's hives, blackberries, and the first katydid. Simon and all of his sons are busy getting in hay between the rains, and the wheat harvest is pretty much in full swing. Edna and her three daughters will soon be busy canning green beans in a hot kitchen. Fresh vegetables are coming in from the garden. Those kitchen gardens are central to the self-sufficiency that the Amish still strive to achieve. Sweet corn and early tomatoes are starting to appear on dinner tables.

August already hints of autumn. Edna and the girls are canning pickles and peaches, and making relish and other garden things. "Garden goodies are such a treat!" she writes. "We've been using tomatoes for several weeks. We picked a couple cantaloupes and our first watermelon yesterday. Beans are being canned. Ivan is taking honey off his hives. He is stacking the supers in the greenhouse to get the honey warm enough to extract. Before we know it fall will be here. The crickets are singing more and more, a sign of late summer." The end of August brings hotter weather and shorter days. It also marks the beginning of school with a work frolic to spruce up the schoolhouse.

September has a smell of its own. "And that smell is apples!" Edna says. Trees in the Yoder apple orchard have branches that are so loaded with fruit they are nesting on the grass.

October is an almost perfect month on the Yoder farm. The cool nights have eliminated bothersome flies, which makes the cows happier. October brings corn harvest, cider making, apple butter—and colors and serenity that only this month can offer. Apple fritters, too! "Along about the middle of the month," Simon says, "we hear a sound that we've been waiting for—the quacking and gabbling of migrating ducks and geese." As the month draws to a close, so does Simon's field work.

November and December are the time to tackle the messier job of butchering meat. The Yoders keep some livestock to provide fresh meat for their family. It's also wedding season, when fields rest and there is time to devote to weddings. This year, the Yoders' oldest son, Glen, is planning to marry.

Winter is a time of cozy fires; eating popcorn and peeled apples; quilting, reading, and playing games in the evenings; snowball fights and sleigh rides. The Yoders are stocking their icehouse.

"The deer become very bold in winter," Simon says. "Their tracks crisscross everywhere around the barn, but not far into the haymow. They're still too wary to act like domestic animals. No doubt, their boldness is increased by the handouts of ear corn the boys have been treating them with."

On the first breakfast of the New Year, Simon prays a special prayer, a family tradition: "Another year is dawning, dear Father. Let it be, on earth or else in Heaven, another year with Thee."

Section Three

Daily Bread

If God is not first in our thoughts in the morning, he will be last in our thoughts all day.

Amish Proverb

Five-year-old Laura is just learning to read. Early one summer morning, Laura woke before everyone else. Her grandmother found her sitting on the couch beside her three-year-old brother, Marcus, with a Bible open on her lap, trying to read from the book of Ezekiel. She was warning her wide-eyed little brother about living creatures and wheels with faces . . . things far beyond their comprehension. But one thing Laura does understand—the day begins with time spent with God's Word.

To the Amish, the wheel of life spins around faith. There's a reason they dress Plain and live simply—to honor God. Amish children like Laura and Marcus grow up with daily Bible readings, prayer, regular church, schooling that affirms the home's beliefs, and a community that upholds God's ways. Something as simple as grace before a meal is part of the tapestry that weaves an Amish life. "We pray before and after every meal," said Old Order Amish bishop Daniel Miller. "The children know when the meal is over, because of that prayer. We give thanks, then we return thanks. We have a Bible reading every morning. Each evening, we ask God's forgiveness for any sins we might have committed during the day. It builds in ready confession. And it adds structure to our lives."

Bookending a day in prayer was how Daniel was raised. "I remember my grandfather offering a memorized prayer, but we have silent prayer."

Bibles, said Erik Wesner, author of *Success Made Simple*, are ever-present in Amish homes. "When I visit Amish friends, a daily morning reading after breakfast was and is the norm. I've often discussed Bible stories, people, and ideas with Amish people, outside of church." But it isn't just an academic activity for the Amish; real faith involves doing. Living by example is the backbone of Amish tradition.

As minister Henry Glick said, "I think of the Bible as a handbook for everyday life. It addresses everything we need to know about how to live, either directly in words or indirectly through example." Everything the Amish do, from chores at home to weddings and funerals, is carried out in a way that shows the young people how it's done—including faith.

There is a saying among them: "People may doubt what you say, but they will believe what you do." Whatever the Amish teach their children, they back up with their actions. "There's no point in knowing God's Word if you don't walk God's Word," Henry said.

The Amish know they are being observed—by their children, by neighbors, by the world. Even little Laura has a younger sibling watching her: Marcus, a three-year-old who has already been introduced to the book of Ezekiel.

God Doesn't Make Mistakes

My job is to take care of the possible and trust God with the impossible.

Amish Proverb

L ess than a year after Barbara Weaver had her eleventh child, she became a widow. Her husband, Milo, passed away after a four-year battle with cancer. Barbara was left to raise eleven children, three of whom were under the age of four. "When Milo was first diagnosed with cancer," Barbara said, "we knew this cancer was a bad one. When I became pregnant with my youngest, I remember thinking, 'Why would God give me another baby if I can't have my husband to raise them?' Milo would tell me, 'God doesn't make mistakes. The time will come when you'll be thankful for these little ones.'"

It's been thirteen years since Milo passed. "He was so right," Barbara said. "These three young ones bring me so much joy, add so much life to the house. At the time, it was hard. It hasn't always been easy. I've had my struggles to work through."

When Milo was diagnosed with cancer, the couple was told to go directly to the hospital to start chemotherapy. "But we didn't want to be hasty," Barbara said. "We wanted to go home and pray first." Afterward, they decided to start chemotherapy, but his tumor was growing rapidly. "The tumor did go away, and he was in remission for a while, but his blood count never went up"—medical code that meant the cancer wasn't gone.

Milo and Barbara prepared for what lay ahead. "We sold our farm and sold our cows. We bought a small property. Others helped us build a house. We had no yard, no barn, no nothing! For a year, Milo was doing well. He told me he even forgot he'd been sick. He built our barn. But then, at a school picnic one May, he noticed something wasn't right. He tried to play ball, but his coordination wasn't right. He couldn't swing a bat. The doctors found the cancer was in his bone marrow. They told us that we could probably do a bone marrow transplant to prolong his life. We decided not to try the bone marrow transplant. Milo went downhill fast. Soon he needed a walker. By October, he was in so much pain that he had no desire to live."

Not much later, Milo passed away.

Barbara remembered that at the time of Milo's funeral, people told her she was lucky to have all of those children at home. "Lucky?! I thought. To raise all these children alone? But now I can see what they meant. At the time, it was overwhelming. But these were older people and had a better perspective of loss, of carrying on."

A Bible verse in the book of Isaiah has helped to anchor Barbara during difficult times: "Thou wilt keep him in perfect peace, whose mind is stayed on thee: because he trusteth in thee" (Isaiah 26:3 KJV). "In order to have that perfect peace, we need to trust God fully and wholly at all times," she says. "Because I am so human I need to remind myself of this daily. However impossible and complicated things may seem to me, 'with God all things are possible.'"

This whole experience—widowhood and raising children on her own—has proven to Barbara that the Lord has been faithful.

"It hasn't always been easy. I've had my struggles to work through. But we can trust him! He's going to look out for you. Trust him!"

ROAD MAP: GETTING THERE FROM HERE

Imagine finding yourself widowed, with eleven children to raise, three under the age of four! Barbara felt thoroughly inadequate as she faced such a daunting task, but she did know she had to depend on God. "Because I am so human I need to remind myself of this daily," she said. "However impossible and complicated things may seem to me, 'with God all things are possible.'" Parenthood can be overwhelming—with one child or eleven! The next time you are feeling inadequate, remember Barbara's testimony. She learned that when her strength was gone, God's strength was sufficient (2 Cor. 12:10).

At her husband's funeral, people reminded Barbara that she would be blessed by those young children. At that moment, she felt anything *but* blessed. But later, she knew they spoke from the wisdom of experience. Our children don't always act like blessings, but from God's perspective, they are! Today, thank God for the blessing of your child.

The Amish believe in the sovereignty of God in all matters. "You have hedged me behind and before, and laid Your hand upon me" (Ps. 139:5 NKJV). Faith in the sovereignty of God can give you confidence as you face difficulties in your life. As Barbara discovered, he will give the strength we need (Phil. 4:13).

In their own words . . .

It wasn't until quite late in life that I discovered how easy it is to say "I don't know."

—Scribe from Redding, Iowa

I heard a story recently about a father who was giving his son good advice concerning productive work and prosperous living. "It's the early bird that gets the worm, you know." "Yes, I know," said the son, "but what about the poor worm? He was up early, too." Dad, too quick to be outwitted, replied, "He was on his way home after staying out too late."

—Scribe from Long Island, Virginia

Gas Thieves

Instead of putting others in their place, put yourself in their place.

Amish Proverb

Although no longer Amish, Mary Ann Kinsinger has fond memories of her childhood. So much so that she started a popular blog called *A Joyful Chaos*, in which she shares memories about growing up Amish in Somerset County, Pennsylvania. One story, in particular, is an example of how Amish parents shape their children. Values—such as turning the other cheek—are taught by example.

Since Daddy had started a woodworking shop, he had bought several fuel tanks and set them up under our pine trees behind the house. He allowed us children to paint the tanks with a shiny silver paint. Once they were dry, he wrote "GAS" on one in big black letters so it wouldn't be confused with the tank of diesel fuel standing right next to it.

It took quite a lot more diesel than gas to run the machinery in Daddy's woodworking shop. Somehow the gas tank always emptied before the diesel tank. Daddy asked all of us if we had opened the valves, or if we had any idea why the tank was already empty. But we were all clueless about what could be happening to the gas.

Once a month, Daddy kept having to refill the gas tank. Then winter came. One morning we woke up to find fresh tracks in the snow right in front of the gas tank. Daddy wasn't very happy about the idea that someone was stealing gas. He decided he was going to try to watch the tank and catch the thieves in the act.

Sure enough, several nights later as Daddy peeped out the kitchen window, he saw our neighbors' two teenage boys filling their gas cans. He hurried down to the basement and out through the shop. He stopped in the engine room just long enough to pick up our gas can.

He walked up to the teenage boys and said, "Here's some more gas you can have." The boys jumped and turned around to see who was there. Daddy repeated, "Here is another can of gas for you." He held out the can to them. They stammered around a bit and refused to accept it.

The boys offered to pay for the gas in their cans, but Daddy refused to take any of their money. He told them the next time they really needed gas to come to the house and he would be glad to give them whatever they needed.

Daddy said goodnight to the boys and came back into the house. The boys stood there awhile and then walked home with their gas. But from that night on, we never had any problems with gas disappearing. And the boys never came to accept Daddy's offer of free gas either.

ROAD MAP: GETTING THERE FROM HERE

Mary Ann's father responded to the gas thieves in a way that was consistent with his principles—as a Christian, as an Amishman. His decision-making process was in place—those principles were his plumb line. Name two or three principles (honesty, for example) that could serve as your plumb line for decision making.

Confrontations are so hard! In one size or shape, they're part of everyone's life. Most of us avoid confrontations at all cost, or bungle the job. Mary Ann and her brothers were given a lesson in how to handle a confrontation to bring about a positive conclusion for all. They observed their father holding the gas thieves accountable for their actions while giving them an opportunity to change their ways. A couple of noteworthy points about Mary Ann's father: he didn't respond to the gas thieves in holy outrage, or without having done due diligence, and he treated them as the young men he hoped they could be. His wise handling of the situation became a living sermon to his children.

In their own words . . .

There's a supposedly true story of the Amishman who took a horse to an auction and gave this horse a good recommendation. An Englishman bought the horse, and some time later came to this Amishman's home as he was not happy with his purchase. He asked to borrow the Amishman's clothes, as he wanted to pawn the horse off on someone else! A compass always points north. Do we Plain people? I'm thinking I have room for improvement.

—Scribe from West Union, Ohio

Sitting on the Front Bench

*When a man won't listen to his conscience, it's usually because
he doesn't like taking advice from strangers.*

Amish Proverb

S itting on the front bench" has a meaning of its own for the
Amish. That is where someone is asked to sit in church when
they're in trouble and need to make a public confession for
wrongdoing.

Such was the case of Tommy B. and Nathan R. On a chilly November evening, Tommy and Nathan, both on the sunny side of
twenty, decided to play a trick on the schoolteacher. They crept
onto the roof of the schoolhouse and covered the chimney pipe
with branches. The plan was that the schoolteacher, Mary Alice,
would arrive at school before the scholars, start the fire, and find
herself in a smokeout. Just a harmless little prank.

Things didn't unfold quite the way the boys had planned.

Mary Alice was late to school the next morning because her
horse threw a shoe. The scholars were already in the schoolhouse,
shivering in the cold room, so one boy decided to go ahead and light
the stove to warm up the room. He scrunched paper into balls and

carefully stacked the kindling on top. He found the matches that Mary Alice guarded in her top desk drawer, struck one, and lit the paper under the wood. Snapping and crackling, the fire grew within the belly of the stove, so the boy closed and latched the steel door.

By now, the room was full of scholars with no sign of Mary Alice. It was too cold to play outside—the kind of cold that took your breath away and froze your cheeks if you stepped outside. So the children sat at their desks or gathered in circles to talk, waiting for their teacher to show up.

A steady stream of thick black smoke started to curl from the stove. At first, the scholars were so absorbed in their unexpected free time that they didn't notice it, but soon dark, smelly smoke rolled through the room. One girl screamed, then another and another. The children panicked and fled outside.

Mary Alice arrived at the schoolhouse in time to see her scholars bursting out of the front door, smoke trailing behind them. She looked up to the roof to spot the source of the problem, then climbed up on the roof herself and knocked the branches off the chimney pipe. It was an easy fix, but the classroom was left with the sour stench of smoke, and the whitewashed walls were tinged with gray.

Tommy and Nathan messed with the wrong teacher. Mary Alice quickly spotted the culprits' handiwork—she found a pocketknife by the woodpile where they cut the branches, with the initials TB carved in the handle. She returned the pocketknife to Tommy, via the bishop.

The bishop suggested that Tommy and Nathan "volunteer" to repaint the interior of the schoolhouse—and to volunteer to pay for the materials too. He also "called" Tommy and Nathan to make a public confession of their deed. The following Sunday, the boys ended up sitting on the front bench. Even though it was mischief with no real harm done, the bishop felt Tommy's and Nathan's confession would serve as an example to the other children sitting in church that day—hopefully deterring them from pranks and foolishness and worse.

Tommy gave a careless shrug after retelling the story about sitting on the front bench. Maybe it was the bravado of youth, but he didn't seem terribly bothered by this moment of public embarrassment. Nathan elbowed him, making him laugh. "Some things are worth a little bit of trouble," Tommy said with a grin.

Road Map: Getting There from Here

One of the benefits of a small community is accountability— much like the concept "it takes a village to raise a child." Tommy and Nathan were held responsible for their actions—something they may not appreciate now, but someday will. What are some ways you can build accountability into your children's lives? Two California moms organized a monthly coffee get-together of the mothers of their children's friends. They met throughout their children's high school years to share ideas about parenting teens. An Oklahoma couple befriended the new youth pastor and his wife at their church. Four years later, the youth pastor offered to write a letter of recommendation for college for their daughter. Accountability isn't always negative! By cultivating some key relationships, you can make a "village" right where you live.

From about four weeks on, infants and children are expected to be in Amish church services. They are tolerated and welcomed, and they grow up with expectations to behave in such an environment. And always, always, Amish children are learning by example. How does that thought change your perspective about segregating children from adults during church services? Consider bringing your children to church—even once a month. Doing so will expose them to hymns, sermons, public prayers, the act of communion. You're preparing them for a lifetime of regular worship.

In their own words . . .

Our daughter, Rosemary, was asked by her daddy which way the egg would roll if a rooster was up on the peak of the roof. She answered by pointing which way. Then we started laughing and told her that roosters don't lay eggs. She piped up, "Well, God can make a miracle happen." Her seriousness and belief in God put us to shame.

—Scribe in Linn, Missouri

Calvin and Goliath

If at first you do succeed, try not to look astonished.

Amish Proverb

I t was a hot August afternoon when a calf supplier pulled into Joe Weaver's farm with some calves on board, including two young bulls on their way to the sale barn for beef. Joe and the calf supplier had to spend some time rearranging the cattle trailer to unload the calves. Either a hinge came undone or a door hadn't been closed tightly—the men aren't sure which—but one of the young bulls decided he had no interest in going to the sale barn. He broke through the small opening, headed for the road, and trotted up to the neighboring Millers' farm.

Calvin Miller, age thirteen, spotted the young bull from his barn and tried to chase him back to the Weavers', but the bull wasn't intimidated by this skinny reed of a boy. It charged Calvin. Joe watched as the bull bumped and pushed Calvin, then practically trampled him. Joe yelled to get the bull's attention. Agitated, it turned away from Calvin and started to charge toward Joe.

Calvin rose to his feet and limped into the barn. The calf supplier tried to help Joe coax the bull into a fenced pasture, but the young bull grew increasingly angry. "So our next big idea," Joe said, "was to stay out of sight until we came up with a better plan." Once or twice, Joe would cautiously come out in the open, but the bull would charge him. "This was one angry bull! I was just about ready to run back to my farm and grab my shotgun when Calvin slipped out of the barn, calm as could be."

The bull spotted Calvin and started to charge, but the boy was ready. He threw a stone, hard, to scare it away and hit the bull's forehead, spot-on. "The stone must have hit that bull at just the right place, because down it went, just like Goliath!" Joe said. At first, Calvin and Joe and the calf supplier remained still, watching. They figured the bull was just knocked out or dazed. "Slowly, we approached the bull and were surprised to find it was dead as a doornail."

Afterward, folks were congratulating Calvin and slapping him on the back, but he only shrugged it off. "A mad bull on the farm is nothing to joke about."

Joe felt differently. "Now Calvin has a modern-day David and Goliath tale to tell his children and grandchildren when he grows up." He smiled a big toothy grin. "All's well that ends well."

ROAD MAP: GETTING THERE FROM HERE

Joe not only affirmed Calvin's bull's-eye pitching skills, but he likened it to the story of David and Goliath. He put Calvin's bravery into a wider context than just quick thinking during an emergency on a farm. Don't be tentative about putting events in your child's life into a broader context—you and your children have a bookmarked place in God's story!

Look for practical ways to make the Bible relevant to your children. One Illinois mom writes encouraging Scripture verses on index cards and customizes them by substituting her children's names. She slips the note into a lunch bag, leaves it on a pillow, or tapes it to the bathroom mirror. When her son was taking the SATs, for example, she wrote out: "We can be confident that what God has started in Tyler's life, He will certainly finish" (see Phil. 1:6). A Texas dad chose life verses for his two daughters and put them on the computer as screen savers—a credo for each child. Such meditations become a constant reassurance of your family's true identity.

In their own words...

One boy was told by his mother to get the bath water ready. A tub was set out behind the house in the afternoon with water in it so the sun would warm it and be ready in the evening. Well, sometime during that sunny afternoon the pig found it and got itself a good bath.

—Scribe from Hartshorn, Missouri

Happy moments—praise God. Difficult moments—seek God. Quiet moments—worship God. Painful moments—trust God. Every moment—thank God.

—Scribe from Hadley, Pennsylvania

Widow Maker

To return good for good is human; to return good for evil is divine.

Amish Proverb

Sixteen-year-old Aaron King was riding his bicycle home from work one November afternoon when he braced himself for the hardest part of his ride: pedaling up Widow Maker on the County Road. Widow Maker is a steep, narrow peak with no shoulder room on the sides of the road. Aaron had to weave around the washouts from the recent rains and hoped there wouldn't be any vehicles trying to get around him. The road was so narrow that most cars or trucks, if they encountered a buggy or a biker on Widow Maker, would stop or slow down.

Most would. But not a certain school bus driver. This driver was known for having a sour attitude toward the local Amish. Whenever he passed a buggy on the road—any road—he wouldn't slow down or make room. "He's just a guy who doesn't care," said Aaron. "He doesn't care what kind of a problem he makes for other folks."

Aaron's mother, Rosanna, was convinced that this bus driver's attitude had rubbed off on the children on the bus. "Those children stick their heads out the windows and yell nasty things at our buggies."

On the rainy afternoon when Aaron was biking home, the school bus charged past him, spitting up water from the puddles. Aaron was prepared for skirting out of the way of the bus, but he wasn't prepared for getting hit by a stone—so hard that it caused a gash on his forehead.

At first, Aaron thought the stone was kicked up by the bus's wheels. "I looked around, just to be sure. I found the stone that hit me. It was completely dry." As he recalled the event, he revealed a large stone, about the size of a small fist. On Aaron's forehead was a scar, evidence of the wound that had been knit together with six black stitches.

"Someone opened the window of the bus and threw it at him," Rosanna said with certainty. "It's a sad thing when schoolchildren think it's funny to throw things at an innocent person who is just biking, minding his own business. And even more sad when they learn their behavior is permissible from an adult." She crossed her arms across her chest. "Ever since that happened, my husband and I sure do turn the burner up on the prayer line when we know Aaron is on his way home."

So what's next? The Kings certainly have cause and enough evidence to go and speak to the school district about the bus driver's behavior.

Rosanna and Aaron exchanged an uncomfortable look, sharing the same thought. "Our Christian duty is to forgive him. And to pray for him." Rosanna walked over to the window and pointed to a small house down the road. "Besides, he's our neighbor."

ROAD MAP: GETTING THERE FROM HERE

Rosanna and Aaron had every right to hold a grudge, but they turned it over to prayer and let it go. Why? Because they knew that they needed to forgive whatever grievances they may hold against people (*especially* difficult people!) just as Christ had forgiven them. It's a core belief of the Amish to extend forgiveness to others and allow God to right the wrongs. But that attitude isn't just for the Amish—it pertains to all Christians (Luke 11:4).

The Amish seem to do a better job with forgiveness than the rest of us, who live in a culture that demands fairness and justice. True forgiveness is an unnatural act, while not forgiving is our first response. Without God's help, we can't do it—not in a lasting, genuine way. But with him, all things are possible (Phil. 4:13). Even for someone who hurts our child's feelings. Or worse, like that bus driver.

One of the reasons the Amish forgive readily is because of their emphasis on humility. It's easier to give others the benefit of the doubt when we remember how prone we are to daily failure, how no one is without sin (Isa. 64:6). We have so much to be forgiven for! For that reason alone we should cultivate an attitude of forgiveness in our homes and in our lives. And thank God that he never gives up on us!

In their own words . . .

On Friday there were five or six work days. Ours was at Lavern B's. The women cleaned the garden, made noodles, washed windows, did some canning. Some of us men folk laid blocks for their barn, while others mowed weeds and did some other odd jobs. We believe it is important to not only get together on Sundays, but also learn to work with each other during the week. Sometimes we may know what each other's names are, but do we really know each other? This reminds me of when a family moved in from the same community that we had lived in. When we were unloading their truck, I asked one of their little boys if he knew who I was. He promptly answered, "No!" I then asked him if he knew my name. Again he promptly answered, "Sam C.!" Now this may sound rather amusing, but might there be something to learn of this innocent statement? As brothers in the church we know each other's names, but might not truly know each other.

—Scribe from Uniontown, Ohio

Northern Lights

A memory is a treasure that survives.

Amish Proverb

Winter felt different. Winter evenings, especially, felt different from any other time of year. And Friday evenings were the best of all. Those are Carolyn Yoder's memories of winter on her family's farm in Ontario, Canada.

Carolyn and her brother Atlee liked to hurry home from school and enjoy the snack that their mother, Nancy, would have waiting for them. "Most of the time it was homemade bread, spread with butter and sprinkled with sugar," Carolyn said, "but on Fridays she would bake cookies for us. Still warm from the oven, they'd be waiting for us as we ran through the door."

After the two children had eaten their snacks, they would hurry to finish their chores. The wood box had to be filled with enough wood to last until the next evening, and then Carolyn would help her mother prepare supper.

On most winter evenings, once the family had eaten and the dishes were washed and put away, Carolyn's mother would send the two children down to the basement with a flashlight and a bowl to get apples from the storage bin. They would all sit around the kitchen while their mother peeled apples and their father read stories aloud. Then Carolyn and her mother would sew while Atlee and their father played checkers or worked on a puzzle. "When the grandfather clock in the hallway clanged eight o'clock," Carolyn said, "Dad would pack up the checkers game. Then we'd come together in the living room to kneel for prayer. Dad would read the evening prayer from his little black prayer book."

Afterward, Carolyn and her brother Johnny would race each other upstairs. Shivering in their unheated bedrooms, they changed into nightclothes and brushed their teeth by flashlight. In the meantime, their mother tucked hot baked potatoes—wrapped in dishtowels—in their beds to warm them up. Carolyn would snuggle deep under the covers, lulled to sleep by the murmur of her parents' voices as they talked downstairs.

One year, the Yoder family took the train to visit relatives who lived in Alberta. "The first night we were there, we had a big dinner and played some board games. My mother had just eyed the clock and gently hinted that she thought a warm bed and a good night's sleep was starting to sound pretty good. Suddenly, my uncle Eli jumped up and said, 'Let's go out on the lake and watch the northern lights.'"

Adventure got the best of them. "My brother Johnny and my dad practically jumped into their boots before Eli finished making that offer." Minutes later, the family started on their way down the path to the frozen lake. "In the dark, as the men started out on the snow-covered ice, I began to feel more than a little anxious, wondering if the ice would hold up. I nearly turned back. I wanted to! But Atlee and my cousins laughed at me."

Carolyn's uncle explained to her that the ice was solid, at least four feet thick. "Eli led the two families, single file, a good ways out on the lake. There we stood and watched the northern lights." Carolyn paused, and the look on her face changed as the wisp of a

#300 07-03-2018 05:34PM
Item(s) checked out to 234100025530255.

TITLE: Amish values for your family : wh
BARCODE: 33410011232420
DUE DATE: 07-17-18

Porter County Public Library
Renew: 531-9054, pcpls.org, or PCPLS app

memory played in her mind. "I watched the brilliant green lights dance across the sky. Behind us, to the south in the pitch black sky above the shoreline, it appeared there were at least a zillion twinkling stars. It was the single most spectacular experience of my entire life. I felt as though my whole life was spent in preparation of this moment. The beauty of God's handiwork brought tears to my eyes. I'll never, ever forget it."

ROAD MAP: GETTING THERE FROM HERE

What special childhood memory do you have of observing something remarkable in the natural world? What made that memory stick? Probably a sense of awe. It's easy to lose that awe as we get older and busier. We miss the miracles that go on around us! A spectacular sunset, a star-studded sky, the short-lived blossoms of a fruit tree in spring. Children have a way of reminding us to pay closer attention to the world and its daily miracles.

Make a habit of noticing nature's miracles. Point out to your children these hints of heaven's grandeur that surround them. "Do you see? You live in God's kingdom—there are signs all around you. He is all around you. And do you realize who you are? You are God's child!"

In their own words . . .

On April 20 [2010], the people who weren't in bed by ten o'clock got to see the flying meteor. It was such an awesome sight, and the rumble that followed sounded like a huge freight train! God moves in mysterious ways His wonders to perform.
—Scribe from Beetown, Wisconsin

It seems after the January thaw, we are having snow flurries—two and a half inches on Friday, [February] 5th. The fields look brighter with snow on the ground than when it's bare. The snow brings the feathered friends to the patio door. They seem to enjoy their smorgasbord. The tame rabbit will come and stand on his hind legs to look in the door, as if to say "Where is my corn?" As soon as we pitch some out there, he's there to enjoy it. There is a snow bird that comes every winter to share the corn with the other winter birds. This snow bird has one white feather in its tail; therefore, we know it's the same one. This is the third winter it has shown up.

—Scribe from Skidmore, Missouri

A Rare Bird

By perseverance the snail reached the ark.

Amish Proverb

E arly on the morning of September 12, 2009, Emery Yoder headed out of his house in Holmes County, Ohio, not far from Berlin, to dig some potatoes but got distracted by the sight of a noteworthy bird in his barnyard—a remarkable, rare bird that few might have noticed. Unless, of course, you're an Amish farmer.

The Amish of Holmes County are known as sharp birders. They've spotted many rare birds that stray onto their farmland. It makes sense that the Amish have a sixth sense for birding: the bulk of their day is spent outdoors, familiar with the nature that surrounds them, and they manage their farms in a wildlife-friendly manner.

This particular bird, a northern wheatear, was making its way to spend the winter in a warmer climate: Africa.

The northern wheatear is a smallish thrush with rather long legs that breeds on the tundra along the northernmost part of North America, above the Arctic Circle. It makes one of the longest journeys of any small bird, crossing desert, ice, and oceans. Every autumn, the birds return to Africa. Only three wheatears have ever been spotted in Ohio.

Emery's rare bird was hanging around a pile of logs in the barnyard. News of the discovery crackled like lightning across the state. Cars started arriving, parking along the dusty rural road. Birders of all ages were gathered beside the driveway, all peering through scopes and binoculars in the same direction.

"This was too good to pass up," says Cheryl Harner, an environmental activist who has a blog called *Weedpicker's Journal*. "It was a beautiful day! We scurried down the back county roads, carefully dodging Amish buggies. It was easy enough to find with the line of cars parked at the end of the drive. The yard had several hired vans and many bicycles along with the horse-drawn wagons. Hundreds and hundreds of people could have passed by that bird and never thought twice. It was very nondescript, and it wasn't at a feeder. This bird is an insect eater. But an Amish farmer noticed an unusual bird in his field. He *noticed!*"

The wheatear was perched atop a woodpile and seemed to enjoy the attention. An excited buzz of birder chatter went up whenever it hopped to a new spot, gobbled up an insect, pumped its tail, or flicked its wings.

"We gathered quietly in a line," Cheryl said, "all thirty or so wheatear admirers, and in hushed tones we compared notes on the soft coloring, white rump, and tail band when it flew from the open ground, where it had foraged for insects, to its favorite log pile. Watching the birders was almost as much fun as watching the bird. Rows of Amish men with long beards, straw hats, and bib overalls mixed with groups of English—non-Amish—who had converged on the site from Cleveland, Akron, Columbus, Mansfield, Toledo, Cincinnati, and Pittsburgh. People were quiet, respectful, happy. Folks were on their best behavior and very appreciative of being welcomed onto the farm."

The bird was obviously not afraid of humans, probably because it hadn't seen any before. It flew within five feet of people to snatch insects. Emery said he hand-fed crickets to the bird. The bird always watched him for his offerings. It would come for a handout as many times as it was offered a cricket.

The bird provided family entertainment for the Amish as horses and buggies arrived and departed throughout the day, and dozens of bicycles rested in the grass. Barefoot Amish boys and Amish girls in dark-colored dresses lent an air of joy to the exciting event.

Emery graciously welcomed all the people who came to his farm to see the bird. He had a tablet for people to sign their names and addresses. "The Amish aren't prideful," Cheryl says. "It's common to have a note pad and ask people to sign it. Having that guest book was Emery Yoder's way of expressing hospitality. English birders have developed a warm relationship with the Amish. The Amish realize that we respect the bird. I think that by opening their farms to bird-watchers, the Amish see it as sharing creation with those who don't share the faith."

Before the wheatear continued its journey, 581 people from six states, including from as far away as South Carolina, came to see the bird. Hundreds of people drawn to see one rare bird!

"This scenic farm and its kind owner was an idyllic place for a bird," says Cheryl. "And it was only out of respect for Amish preference that I didn't photograph the many Amish and English gathered there. Black hats or birding T-shirts, we are all the same in the presence of a great bird."

ROAD MAP: GETTING THERE FROM HERE

"An Amish farmer noticed the presence of an unusual bird in his yard," said Cheryl. "He *noticed*!" What do you learn from that?

Reverence for God's creation is a cardinal value of the Amish. "They're so patient," Cheryl said. "Other birders will use bird calls or their iPods to draw birds out—not even caring that they might be stressing the birds. But the Amish will wait patiently, until the bird is ready to appear." How does such patience display a reverence?

Why does living in harmony with nature reflect an appropriate humility toward God? One Washington state family has stopped using man-made chemicals on their lawn after growing concerned about run-off into a nearby creek. An Oregon family left a small section of their grape arbor uncovered, food for a flock of wild turkeys that roamed their neighborhood. A family in Michigan didn't use their back door all spring because a bird had built a nest in the eave above it. What is one step your family can take to better care for the natural world around you?

In their own words . . .

Yard sales are in full swing again, and what lady doesn't enjoy them? I'm always pleased when I find decent boots, shoes, and clothes for the family, especially when they're cheap. Yesterday I found a telescope with a tripod for a dollar all in the box yet like it was never used. Were my boys ever pleased! They were hoping the clouds would allow the moon to show through so they could look at it. After dark, they set it up in the yard and enjoyed looking at the moon. One of the children ran in and said that they saw the Creator in the moon. I wouldn't have minded seeing the Creator either, but they really meant crater.

—Scribe from Liberty, Kentucky

Seventy Times Seven

Some may see a hopeless end, but as believers we rejoice in an endless hope.

Amish Proverb

*I*ntrigued. That's the word to describe how Dr. Bryan Cloyd, professor of accounting at Virginia Tech in Blacksburg, Virginia, felt when he learned that a busload of Amish from Nickel Mines, Pennsylvania, was coming to honor the victims of the April 2007 school shootings. Dr. Cloyd's only daughter, Austin, age eighteen, was one of thirty-two victims who lost their lives in the rampage. "When I heard that the Amish were coming," he said, "I started to learn all I could about them, about how they were able to forgive. I was looking forward to meeting them. I wanted to explore how they were able to come to forgiveness so quickly that day."

The purpose of the Amish visit was to bring the Comfort Quilt to Virginia Tech. After the 9/11 terrorist attacks in New York City, a school in Ohio created a simple patchwork quilt for children whose parents had been killed in the attacks. A school in New Jersey hung the quilt, and there it stayed—until four years later, when Hurricane Katrina hit New Orleans. The Comfort Quilt was sent to a school in Mississippi that had taken in many displaced New Orleans students. When the Nickel Mines School shooting occurred, the Comfort Quilt moved again . . . this time to bring comfort to the Amish families of Nickel Mines. After the Virginia Tech tragedy, the Amish made a decision that the quilt should be moved again.

"I spent a couple of hours before that lunch meeting really thinking about what I wanted to say, to ask," Dr. Cloyd said. "I was trying to write a short letter or note thanking the community for coming to visit with us, for bringing the quilt. Sometime in the course of thinking that through and writing that letter, I came to some peace myself. I realized that Austin was in heaven. And if she was in heaven, she could not be angry. If she wasn't angry, then I shouldn't be angry either."

During the visit, Dr. Cloyd had conversations with some of the Amish fathers. "I remember one of the fathers telling me that forgiveness is a process, not a single point in time. And while it was wildly publicized in the media how quickly the Amish came to forgiveness—certainly what was written was true—but even for them, he said, it was a continual process. When Jesus told Peter to forgive seventy times seven, this Amish father said he now understood that as a process. Not only for repeated actions but perhaps even for the same thing."

After the lunch, the Amish were taken to the memorial that had been erected on campus for the victims. "They were very interested in seeing each of the stones. They had some familiarity with each of the names. It didn't surprise me that they knew the names. I strongly suspect they prayed for each of us, by name. I'm *sure* they did."

Dr. Cloyd's relationship with these Amish families didn't end there. "I met with them in October 2007 in Pennsylvania, at the home of one of the families who had lost a daughter. They were having a one-year community gathering and were gracious enough to invite us." Dr. Cloyd has kept in touch with some of those Amish fathers. "I keep hoping to have a men's retreat between our church and the Amish. I think it would be useful for the men of our church. The influence of the Amish, the example of their obedience, their faith, would really challenge us and bring us closer to God. I would love to have that men's retreat with them."

It's been said that when parents lose a child, their life is shaped into two halves: before and after. Dr. Cloyd struggled to find meaning in life after Austin's death. "On that morning in April, I was at my desk doing what I thought was important. Two buildings over, my daughter was killed."

It was in his process of finding some meaning in life that Dr. Cloyd came upon the opportunity to go to Haiti. While there, he learned that a remote village was in dire need of a school. *That*, he knew, was something he could do to help. Through his church in Virginia, he was able to provide the financial support to build and maintain a small school for that village. "It's been a real joy to see it come together so quickly. The school began classes on October 12, 2009, so it was up and running by the time of the earthquake on January 12, 2010. We were able to take in twenty of the refugee children from Port au Prince." Today, there are 190 students in the school.

Dr. Cloyd has no doubt that God led him to Haiti. A bonus is the many similarities he's observed between the Haitians and the Amish. "A simpler life, a focus on family and community." For him, he has found meaning in life through this experience of service. "It's been the ultimate ability to rediscover joy. It's very hard to feel joyful if you don't feel there's meaning to your life. But joy comes—when you're doing something with your life and feeling that you're responsive to God's call."

ROAD MAP: GETTING THERE FROM HERE

True forgiveness is never easy, and the Amish struggle with the same emotions of anger and retribution that we all do. But they choose to forgive—with no strings attached—in spite of those feelings. Forgiving is woven deep into their culture. It is not a choice; it is an expectation. The Amish forgive because they believe God's way is the best way to live. They believe forgiveness is intended for our own good. How does that concept help you?

Is there someone you are struggling to forgive today? Having an intention of forgiveness can help to change your feelings about forgiving someone who has wronged you. Try to pray, each day, for that individual. If you have trouble with that, ask someone who understands the situation to pray for you. Don't give up if you don't feel anything. It might take time—but the intention to forgive remains steadfast. Remember Dr. Cloyd's discovery: "Forgiveness is a process."

Dr. Cloyd found healing and joy in serving others. Look for someone you can serve this week. Make a meal for a sick friend, offer extra carpool help to a frazzled mom, babysit for a couple so they can have some uninterrupted time. Joy comes in caring for others.

In their own words . . .

We had a special day of fellowship with folks who had lost a child or loved one. Bishop Enos K. was asked to speak on the loss of a son in an accident, and John F. of Nickel Mines was asked to speak on their community's experience in the Nickel Mines School tragedy of 2006. Tears flowed freely among the audience as he told of the horrors of the shooting . . . but he also spoke of God's grace in the healing of broken hearts and the outpouring of love and support coming from far and near. Here were a group of people who had learned to weep with those that weep and then again to count our blessings and rejoice with those that rejoice. It was a precious afternoon of fellowship amidst alternate sunshine and rain showers.

—Scribe from Millersburg, Pennsylvania

Our hearts were deeply touched and saddened on Friday for the Phil M. family of Strawberry, Arkansas, when their nineteen-year-old son, Travis, collapsed and died. There were several times in past years he passed out . . . but this was the appointed time to respond to the call to "come on home."

—Scribe from Seymour, Missouri

The Miracle of the Neighbor

People don't care how much you know until they know how much you care.

Amish Proverb

One moonless summer night, as the Marvin Schrocks returned home from a singing, they found quite a surprise waiting for them at home. Their yard was full of loose dairy cows and a neighbor's bulls. "Imagine if you can," Elsie Schrock said, "a pitch-black night, huge bulls and about fifty cows all over your yard, driveway, sidewalks, lower beds, garden, new strawberry patch. All the bulls, or most, being as black as the night."

The wandering livestock belonged to the Schrocks' non-Amish neighbor, Jace Koblentz, a man known for being cantankerous. "When Jace Koblentz's big bulls decide to roam, they go wherever they have a mind to," Elsie said. "Jace put up a hot-wire fence to keep his herd in and thinks that's all they need. But these bulls do not respect a flimsy hot tape! Those bulls crossed the road and got our usually calm, tame cows all riled up and wild in a hurry." Fences were quickly broken. "I was worried about how we would ever get them all back into their pens, it being so dark, and the animals were so nerved up. But God was looking out for us. A few other families were all on the way home from the singing and saw the trouble we were in, so they stopped to help."

It wasn't as difficult as Elsie feared. "Once Marvin got in front of the cows and started calling them, it didn't take long to get them back in, the neighbor's bulls and all. The only 'damage' was cow pies all over, nose drippings wiped across the window screens, and a few trampled flowers." Elsie said it was amazing how little damage they actually had. "The worst thing was a few broken fence rails, and our bird feeder poles were bent way over." She shook her head so hard that her cap strings went flying. "I still can't figure out why those bulls wanted bird food."

One week later, it happened again. "Jace's same bulls got out and crossed the busy road, heading toward our corn field!" Elsie said. "Marvin and our boys made some fast tracks to get Jace's herd of bulls behind stronger fences, knowing the havoc these bulls could cause—to go wild and on the loose in this huge corn field. These huge black bovines have been in another neighbor's barn and got into the feed bags. They go wherever they have a mind to."

Elsie described Jace Koblentz as an irate, irresponsible neighbor. "He's been unresponsive to all the patience and forbearance that his Christian neighbors have shown to him over the years." She sighed. "But . . . it's left us feeling thankful again for God's protection."

But then, last fall, something changed. Jace Koblentz changed. "I don't know what happened, but would you believe that such a hard-hearted, angry man started going to church and talking about God? It's like Jace is a new man. Even his face—it's lost that hard stony look." Elsie lifted her hands, as if in praise. "It had to be God's doing. Only God could work a miracle in *that* neighbor!" All the neighbors rejoiced to hear Jace say he's loading those cows and bulls up and sending them off, Elsie said. She raised a thin eyebrow. "Now if he'd only send the dogs along. But that's another story."

ROAD MAP: GETTING THERE FROM HERE

The entire Schrock family worked together to gather up the bulls and return them to their neighbor, Jace Koblentz. Do you ever find yourself not asking for help from your children because it's easier to do it yourself? Farm life probably presents more opportunities to involve children in work or chores, but there are still plenty of ways to get your children working alongside you. Setting the table, taking out the garbage, helping with dishes, cleaning up the yard after a storm, mowing the lawn and raking leaves, shoveling the front path of snow. Next time, ask! The goal is that one day you won't even have to ask. You can expect their help. And as they mature, they will know to help others.

Everyone has some version of a Jace Koblentz in their life. It's easy to write a person like that off and avoid him. God, with his wisdom from above, has a different perspective. Does God ever write someone off? (See Luke 6:35.)

The story of Jace Koblentz is a good reminder to all of us to continue to pray for those who have wronged us, to trust in God for the work of transformation, and—as Elsie did—thank God for his steadfast care and protection.

In their own words . . .

We never used the orange SMV emblem here, and instead used a triangle of gray reflective tape, which actually shows up better than the orange at nighttime. After one of our members received a ticket for not displaying an orange one, a court trial was set. After the judge learned it stemmed from religious convictions, he suggested we have a meeting with the sheriff department and he would delay sentencing till later. In our meeting, the sheriff was quite unwilling to consider our convictions, stating that, "The law is the law, and it is his duty to enforce it." In our quest for a peaceful solution, we learned later that in the 1980s a number of Amish had gone to jail over this issue in North Lawrence County. Legislatures then stepped in, and a NY State Exemption was passed for horsedrawn vehicles if they displayed seventy-two square inches of reflective tape and four red lenses on their lanterns. We wrote the sheriff department a letter informing them of this and humbly asking them to check into this. In a few weeks we received a polite reply that we are correct, and we will no longer receive a ticket for not having an orange emblem. The judge has also dismissed the other cases. For all the sad, sorrowful conditions that exist in our country today, we still owe our Creator the deepest of thanks for the freedom of which we are so unworthy.

—Scribe from Fultonville, New York

Section Four

Letting Go

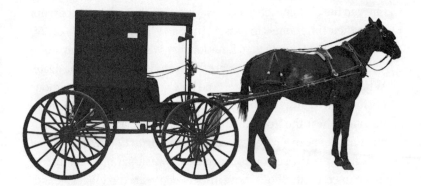

Trouble is easier to get into than out of.

Amish Proverb

L etting go seems to be part of the package of adulthood—
letting go of a toddler's hands as he wobbles away on his own
two legs, letting go of the back of a bicycle seat as a child
pedals away for the first time, letting go of an eighteen-year-old as
he heads off to college, letting go of a daughter on her wedding day.
Or even the ultimate letting go—saying good-bye to elderly parents
when their time comes to pass. Letting go is part of the cycle of life.
Intellectually, we know that. Emotionally? Well, that's another story.

The teen years, in particular, are the hardest for parents to navigate.
When is letting go appropriate? And how do we rein them in without
pushing them away? What parent hasn't laid in bed late at night,
waiting to hear the front door click open. *Ah!* A sigh of relief! Then
and only then can a parent sleep well. *My son (or daughter) is home!*

It might surprise you to learn that Amish parents feel just as
much uncertainty about those in-between years (no longer a child,
not yet an adult) as the rest of us do. Raising teens isn't easy for any
parent. "Teens are really into self," said Daniel Miller, an Old Order
Amish bishop in Holmes County, Ohio. "They're living in an age
of entitlement. I wonder if they will be prepared for the future. I'm
not sure how they will respond to hard times."

Sound familiar to your own inner anxiety about your teen?

In the last few years, I have spoken to many groups about the
Amish. Without fail, someone will bring up Rumspringa. Heads

nod enthusiastically, because it's a subject about which most people are familiar and have strong opinions. Yet Rumspringa is one of the most misunderstood concepts about the Amish.

Rumspringa is a Pennsylvania Dutch word that means—literally— "to run around." When an Amish teen turns sixteen, he is now of age to attend youth gatherings. The amount of freedom a teenager is given varies from family to family, from district to district, even from state to state.

"Rumspringa in Ohio depends a lot on each family, on the kinds of parents," Daniel Miller said. "The majority of parents don't want their kids to go too far. There's not a lot of winking at it. But we know it's part of a period—you take a look at what's out there. And there's not a lot you can do about it. It's risky. I'm not approving of it, not condemning it."

The retention rate of Old Order Amish teens is quite remarkable—85 to 90 percent join the church. Those who don't join usually end up at an Amish-Mennonite church. Contrast that to mainstream teens, raised in the church—over 61 percent do *not* attend church as adults.[1]

Maybe there's something we can learn from the Amish concept of Rumspringa. If we've done our job and prepared our children to the best of our ability, we can let them have a little age-appropriate breathing room to practice decision making, to spread their wings, to learn from mistakes.

And if your child pushes the boundaries of your comfort zone, have mercy on him. Don't give up hope that your values are deeply embedded in your child—there to guide him and help him get back on track. Trust that during times of wandering, doubting, or even out-and-out rebelling, the Lord will pursue him and bring him back (Isa. 43:1). And on that day of return, believe God will do his redeeming miracle and turn your child's heart toward a sincere and lasting love for God (Ps. 119:67, 71). Letting go really means giving over to God.

Bear!

Experience is a different teacher, giving you the test first and the lesson later.

Amish Proverb

Winter in the northern regions is often unwilling to give up its hold, and when spring comes late, even the wildlife can become stressed with a scarcity of food. Such was the winter of 2009. "We've had a lot of bear stories lately," said Ed Graber, who lives in a small settlement in Ontario, Canada. "Black bears are generally nonviolent and peace loving, but we've had some activities lately that have definitely violated this assumption, because some people's peace has been disturbed. Like my wife's peace of mind in our home."

One Sunday morning, a story was told by an upset member of Ed's church. Her dog, Shadow, went missing the night before. Shadow was an old, portly dog that was normally kept on a tie-down in the yard so he wouldn't run off. "A couple of older boys went on a search into the bush to search for Shadow," Ed said. They soon found Shadow's remains. "As they were trying to figure out what had happened, they heard some hissing and growling coming from the nearby bushes. Good judgment prevailed, and further inspection by the boys, thankfully, was immediately forgotten." Ed wasn't there to see the show but said he thought the bear probably watched the boys run off with a big grin, thinking to himself, "Wow, those boys can run fast."

Later that week, about three miles from Ed's house, a fellow saw a black bear eating the bird seed from his bird feeder. The man went out to shoo it away, but quickly changed his mind. He spotted a panther crouched under the pine trees, watching the bear. The man turned around to go to the house and discovered the panther's mate crouched at the corner of his house. He dashed for the door and made it, all in one piece!

The very next day, Ed's son spotted a bear. "Our oldest, Joe, was coming home one evening and saw a bear cross the road, only about a half mile from our farm. His horse came to a dead stop and refused to go on. Joe flashed on the bear with his LED light, which made the bear disappear into the field." Ed thought Joe used good sense.

"These reports have got all of us a little jumpy," Ed said. "I don't worry so much because I know my boys know how to protect themselves, if need be, with guns. But my wife has gotten real antsy. She doesn't want the kids to get too far from the house. She won't let the older boys go out in the evening at all. And she's even making sure the dogs stay in the barn each evening, which breaks those poor dogs' hearts. They like to roam the yard; they like to feel as if they're protecting us. I tell her this is all good experience for everybody, even the dogs, to learn to be wise to nature. I tell her, 'Fannie, you ought not to be worried. Our lives are in God's hands.'"

Road Map: Getting There from Here

Whether the dangers in your world are hungry bears in the backyard or speeding cars on the freeway, life is filled with risk. There's a fine line between taking wise preventative measures and overprotecting our children from every possible threat. That fine line can be discerned by predetermining some principles. For example, one Kansas couple tells their teens, "Nothing good happens after midnight." Their teens can go out on weekend nights, but they have a midnight curfew. A California mom hires a lifeguard for backyard pool parties for her children. The kids can swim and play, but there's an extra pair of trained eyes on the pool.

Husbands and wives often differ in their viewpoint of risk for their children. Fannie wanted the children to stay close to home, safe from danger. Ed had confidence that his sons knew how to protect themselves. The best response is often somewhere in the middle. The next time you and your spouse are at opposite ends on a parenting decision, remember the gift of compromise.

Sometimes, anxieties and "what ifs" can hold us captive, preventing us from enjoying our children's interests and accomplishments and rites of passage. All we see is the risk! We don't see the delight in learning to ride a bicycle or drive a car; we see the danger of collisions. Remember, while we do have to accept the hazards of living, our confidence is in the Lord (Ps. 91:9–11). He never leaves our children for a second (Heb. 13:5).

In their own words . . .

Sam and Mary S. have their chickens running loose. Lately they lost three. This week Mary saw their rooster running fast. She said it looked like he was doing forty miles an hour. The fox was after the hens, and the rooster chased him under the fence, but he again went after the chickens till Mary screamed enough that he left. But he did have some feathers in his mouth!

—Scribe from Lewisburg, Kentucky

Chain Saws and Worries

A word to the wise is unnecessary.

Amish Proverb

Here's another of Mary Ann Kinsinger's childhood reminiscences from her blog, *A Joyful Chaos*. This story is a good reminder that "worry is the worst of imagination."

We used to have a big couch covered with a slippery brown cover that sat underneath our living room windows. John and David, my brothers, and I used to spend a lot of time on it playing church or looking at story books. It also provided an excellent view of the barnyard if we knelt on the seat cushions to look out the windows.

One snowy morning a pickup pulling a cattle trailer drove into the driveway. A man got out and came to the door. Mom went to see what he wanted and then came into the living room. She told us to play nicely while she went out to the barn to help him get our fattened steer loaded into the trailer.

We quickly scrambled onto the couch and watched out the window as Mom walked out to the barn. The man backed his trailer down behind the barn and out of sight of the house. Before long,

Mom and the man appeared, walking to the shop. We were trying to discern what they could want in there when they appeared again. This time, the man was carrying one of Daddy's chain saws. They walked back toward the barn and disappeared behind it.

And then we heard the chain saw.

John and David were contentedly watching out the window for the next time Mom would appear, when I announced—with all my six-year-old authority—that "I think that man is cutting Mom's legs off!" and promptly started to cry.

John and David looked at me, wide-eyed. The thought of Mom having her legs cut off was so overwhelming that they joined me in crying. Howling would describe it better.

We forgot all about watching out the window as we sat on the floor holding each other, crying at the top of our lungs at the dreadful thing that was happening to Mom! All of a sudden, she was standing in front of us demanding to know what was wrong.

Her legs appeared to be fine, and I started to feel sheepish. John had no such problem and announced that I told him the man was cutting her legs off.

Mom seemed flabbergasted with me! She explained that there had been a tree branch in the way that had to be cut so the trailer could be backed up to the barn door.

I think of this episode at times when I am tempted to worry about things. It is a perfect reminder how silly it is to waste time thinking of all the dreadful things that might happen.

ROAD MAP: GETTING THERE FROM HERE

Sometimes our active imaginations can run away from us. Many parents find themselves worrying excessively about their children. Especially when we wake in the night with a jolt. We feel so helpless to keep our children safe from accidents, from evil. How often do you worry about something that is outside of your control? Most things are! But they aren't beyond God's control (Ps. 37:7).

Scripture reminds us that there's no place our children can go where they are outside of God's care (Prov. 3:24–26). Instead of fearing sudden or unseen disasters, we should turn our anxious thoughts to God's sovereignty, to ask for his help. We need to let God manage our fears. In such peace, moms and dads can truly rest.

In their own words . . .

One's imagination can play tricks as one girl found out lately. As she was walking home from the neighbors' after dark, her heart jumped into her throat and her step quickened as she saw these two men sitting beside the road, a red glow in their hands. Out of breath, she rushed into the shop and told her dad, hurry, put out the light! I want to show you something!" When she was through showing him, he calmly told her, "I just got done putting ashes on a pile, and there were a few red coals with it. Calm down, the men are fence posts."

—Scribe from Pleasant Hill, Illinois

Here in America we have so much to be thankful for. In spite of the economic woes we are facing, we are still a blessed nation. Just as some of our parents did in the 1920s, we will just have to ride it out. Throw more beans in the pot or water down the soup and somehow, someway, make ends meet. The forty years that the Israelites wandered in the wilderness, the Lord provided for them, and if we would only put our faith and trust in God, he will do the same for us, no matter how bleak things look now.

—Scribe from Liberty, Kentucky

Pastimes

The right to do something doesn't always make it the right thing to do.

Amish Proverb

One summer evening, there were some anxious moments in a little Wisconsin town at a Sunday singing. A group of young Amish youth had gathered together for a game of volleyball and a supper of barbecued chicken. After everyone had eaten, a few parents stayed around and shuffled everyone into the schoolhouse for the singing. "Lively singing, too," said Mary Emma Gingerich, one of the parents. "We had sung just a few songs when we suddenly heard an ambulance siren going off to the east of the schoolhouse." It wasn't difficult for Mary Emma to figure out where it was headed.

Earlier, as the Amish youth were playing volleyball, some English neighbor boys were going up and down the street on their four-wheelers. "I don't know if they were trying to disrupt us or if they were just showing off," Mary Emma said, "but they would come zooming up the road and hit the curve of the road in front of the schoolhouse, so the four-wheeler would go airborne. There's an incline on the road, and at the speed they were going, they ended up about four to five feet off the ground."

Silence blanketed the room as the ambulance siren abruptly stopped near the schoolhouse. The quiet was soon replaced with the thundering claps of an approaching helicopter. "All it took was for one or two boys to ease toward the open schoolhouse door to see what was going on," Mary Emma said. "Soon everyone dashed outside and down the street to see the helicopter land."

At the accident scene, the Amish saw a teenager on a gurney, thrashing and moaning as he was getting prepared to be transferred to the helicopter. "That boy's legs looked broke like a rag doll," Mary Emma said. "From what we could piece together, he made the jump going extra fast and came down hard. Both he and the four-wheeler went rolling. They ended up quite a ways from the road."

As the helicopter took off, the adults led the Amish youth back to the schoolhouse and tried to get the singing back on track. "The singing wasn't quite as lively after that," Mary Emma said. "I couldn't help but appreciate having our young folks singing instead of being involved with sports that . . . as the Scriptures say . . . 'profit little.'"

Road Map: Getting There from Here

Watching the paramedics carry that boy away on a stretcher is something those Amish children will never forget. While we certainly don't need to be ambulance chasers, we shouldn't avoid exposing our children to the reality of some dangers. Here's an example: The first time fifteen-year-old Tad drove home from school with his newly minted learner's permit, he and his mom passed a car—driven by a teen—that had crashed and flipped over just moments before. A sad observation, but a timely one for Tad. When your children are exposed to grim realities, keep in mind that such exposure might help them recognize preventable dangers.

Recreation can be a good thing. God knows we need refreshment in our life! But sometimes, the good can crowd out the best. Consider your hobbies or pastimes. Where does God fit in the time you spend on those activities?

What pastimes does your family engage in? Are they ones you value? Or are they ones you feel pressed into doing? The world wants to "squeeze us into its mold." Now and then, all of us need to take stock of how we are spending our time. Is the television on a little more than you'd like it to be? Is the computer absorbing your day? Ask God to search your heart and guide you to needed change.

In their own words...

On the east edge of town is a very large cemetery and a casket business next to the road. In front of the store is a large tombstone facing oncoming traffic which reads "Drive with care, we can wait."

—Scribe from Bloomfield, Iowa

A Dog's Life

In youth we learn, in age we understand.

Amish Proverb

I f someone had told Danny and Esther Miller six months ago that they would be in the market for another dog—and glad to make that long trip to town to do it—they never would have believed it. "We had just finished up a litter with old Mollie," said Esther. "Ten puppies tumbling about underfoot just about did me in. After selling or giving away eight pups, we were down to two. Two inseparable puppies that the kids named Jack and Jill. Those two played together from morning till night, chasing each other around the tree, running and pouncing on phantom objects, rolling around in the grass. They provided daily entertainment for our whole family!"

That was pretty significant in itself, Danny said, because he was a farmer through and through. "Animals need to pay for themselves on a farm," he said, "and here I was, finding moments in each day when I would stop and gaze at Jack and Jill, getting the biggest kick out of them." The entire Miller family was enamored of the two growing puppies.

On a sunny August afternoon, the Millers' ten-year-old daughter, Melissa, found her older brothers' BB gun left in the barn. Guns are a part of farm life, and the Miller boys used the BB gun to practice target shooting, plus to thin out the pesky crows that helped themselves to the garden. Melissa took her seven-year-old sister, Melody, out to the far yard, away from the farmhouse and animals, and the two of them shot at a can on the fence. What she didn't realize was how fast Jack and Jill could get into the middle of things. "In their 'play' she shot Jack," said Danny. "When she realized she had killed him, she came running into the house, nearly beside herself. We had to calm her down before we could understand what she was saying."

"Melissa is an animal lover," Esther said. "This nearly broke her heart."

The bottom dropped right out of the world for Jill when she lost her littermate. "She wandered listlessly from one resting place to another, looking dolefully at anyone who stopped to scratch her ears and sometimes barking a half wail, half moan kind of bark," said Esther. "What could we do?"

Danny shrugged. "So the girls talked me into driving over to Lawrence. I heard about a fellow who had some eight-week-old pups he wanted to find homes for."

That afternoon, a new puppy was brought home. Melody held the puppy out for Jill to inspect. "She stretched to sniff the little thing, her whole body quivering. Then her tail began to wag, and she gamboled playfully about, trying to get something started."

That trip to Lawrence paid off, Danny said. "The light has come back into Jill's eyes. But next week when the girls' third pair of flip flops is strewn in little pieces about the yard, and I hear plenty of complaints about it, I may wish I'd left good enough alone." He bent down to scratch Jill's ears.

"That incident became a springboard for us to teach our daughter that guns are not a toy," Esther said. "We were very thankful it was a dog and not her little sister! Neither of us realized a BB gun would kill a dog."

The guns, Danny pointed out, are now securely locked in the gun cabinet.

ROAD MAP: GETTING THERE FROM HERE

En gscheit Hinkel legt aa alsemol newich's Nescht is a Penn Dutch saying that translates to: "Even a clever hen will lay outside the nest." It means that accidents will happen, even in the best of families. Accidents like Melissa had can really shake a child's confidence. The most important part of making mistakes is the lessons we learn from them. The next time your child has (or causes) an accident, try to take it in stride as part of the bumps and bruises of life. See it as something to grow *from*, not something to grow fearful *over*.

Guns are part of most rural families' lives, including the Amish. That knowledge might surprise you. In fact, you might feel critical of it because of what a danger guns can be with young children around. The Amish might point out that cars are quite dangerous too, but that doesn't stop the English from driving them. We face dangers and hazards every day. It's good to remember that God is your family's constant protector (Ps. 34:7). As we trust in God's care, he will take away the fears that grip us in the night and the worries that nag us by day (Ps. 91:4–5).

In their own words . . .

One of our boys thought I should go hunting too. "My place," I said, "is at home, praying for all of you to arrive back safely!" (And also run from window to window with the binoculars when I hear shots!)

—Scribe from Jamestown, Pennsylvania

Did we ever hear of a dog buying a house? The farm sale of the late Ervin and Ann B. was held on Saturday. The house was a Sears Roebuck house and was to be sold and removed from the premises. When they were auctioning it off, they couldn't get a bid. So the auctioneer asked the crowd if someone would take it if he gave it to them. The dog, who had been quiet all day, went "Woof, Woof!" So to speak, the dog bought the house.
—Scribe from Arcola, Illinois

Chuck and Henry and Two Eagles

Greet the dawn with enthusiasm and you may expect satisfaction at sunset.

Amish Proverb

Red warning signs line the fences that surround a picturesque Amish farm in Lancaster County: Restricted Access. There's a large tree on the property with branches that cradle a stick nest the size of a Volkswagen. The tree is home to a pair of nesting bald eagles. Across the street from the farm is Chuck Engle, a kind, older gentleman with a ready smile. Chuck is a retired truck driver turned avid bird-watcher with two large telescopes perched on a hilltop. Flanking Chuck is a thirteen-year-old Amish boy named Henry, with turquoise eyes, a straw hat over his floppy bangs.

The eagles have been living on Henry's family farm for the past five years. Chuck has been politely observing the eagles, from a distance, for those five years. One afternoon, Henry's father asked him if he would like to come on the property and see the nest, up close. Chuck jumped at the chance. A friendship began to develop between Chuck and the family. Chuck was especially fond of Henry, the middle of six boys and one sister, and the one with the keenest interest in birding and wildlife. Henry mows Chuck's lawn, and Chuck does English-style favors for the family—drives them to the doctor, for example. Weather and chores permitting, Henry grabs his scooter and joins Chuck on the hilltop at sunset to watch the eagles.

Henry's father, Chuck says, is a true patriarch. He has an air whistle that he uses to call the kids to the house—a code for each child. "He doesn't raise his voice, but those boys jump when he tells them what to do. One time, I was over there and the dad quietly pointed out, 'Henry, time for the grass to be mowed,' and Henry jumped!" But there is time for fun too. "Once I asked Henry's father if I could take Henry up to a wilderness area for the day, to count birds for migration, and he said, 'Sure!' I ended up taking three of Henry's brothers along too. Had a full day with those boys. A great day."

Another time, Chuck and Henry went alone to the wilderness area. "Henry spotted seventeen separate species of birds and made quick work of it! He's a smart kid." When they returned home, Chuck gave Henry one of his books on bird-watching. "I had four books. I didn't need all of them." He shrugged. "So I gave him the best one."

During the third spring, the eagles had their first eaglet. "They were new parents and didn't know how to care for the young," Chuck said. "The baby died, probably of neglect. We knew something had gone wrong one evening when we saw the mother on the nest's edge—her back was turned toward the nest, and her head was down. The father bird flew in, stroked her neck with his beak. We had tears rolling down our faces. He was clearly consoling her."

Year four went a little better. The eagles raised two eaglets. This spring, year five, they are raising three. Eagles mate for life and live up to thirty years.

The eagles are a sight: females can weigh as much as fourteen pounds with wingspans reaching eight feet; males weigh seven to ten pounds. Their talons are as large as man's hand. These parents rarely leave the nest unattended. The mother feeds her young with trout from the creek that borders the Amish farm. The father is perched in a nearby tree. When she is done feeding her brood, or has had enough of their incessant demands, she hops to the end of a branch, waits a few moments, then takes off into the sky. In swoops the father eagle to babysit the nest. The babies take six months to mature and leave the nest. When they are ready to fly, Chuck explained, they look bigger than the parents because they still have baby feathers under their flying feathers. "The nest that seems large now will get quite crowded."

As the sun lowers along the horizon, the soaring silhouette of the mother eagle is visible in the sky. Chuck peers through a telescope as Henry leans his back against Chuck's car, one ankle crossed over the other. Their eyes are fixed on the eagles.

ROAD MAP: GETTING THERE FROM HERE

The relationship that developed between Chuck and Henry's family was accidental—brought together through a mutual interest in and respect for the bald eagles. Remember that everything that happens to you is first filtered through God's hand. Interruptions can become opportunities. What you might see as accidental or just a coincidence, God might see as a divine appointment. How does such thinking change your perspective on interruptions?

Chuck and Henry have a relationship similar to a grandfather and a grandson. Is there a child or teen or older person in your life who could use some extra attention? Consider doing an activity together that might connect the two of you. You just have to take one step at a time. But it's very possible that, given time, a precious relationship will result.

In their own words . . .

Friday morning the boys came running in, saying there was a bald eagle sitting in our bean field. He was contentedly eating something and came closer and closer. He finally spread his majestic wings and glided into our pasture field, where he perched atop a tree, sunning himself. It is truly wondrous and great how God created each individual insect or bird, just so. Let us not forget to sing him a praise for all his goodness.

—Scribe from Salem, Indiana

Rumspringa

The yoke of God does not fit a stiff neck.

Amish Proverb

Samuel and Hannah Hostetler have five grown children—four of whom have joined the church, married, and started families of their own. All but Matthew, the youngest. "Matthew was just different from the start," Samuel said. "Always questioning. Always restless. He went a little wild during his teen years, and it was extremely painful. We sat the window, at midnight, waiting for him to come home." Samuel is an Old Order Amish bishop.

Matthew is married now, with children, and while he has a good relationship with his parents and siblings, he still hasn't joined the Amish church. "It's not easy," Samuel said. "There's not a lot you can do about it. We need patience. Pray and be patient and be loving. And then we just wait. You know, in the book of Galatians, patience, love, and joy come *before* faith. We have to have patience with our kids. And we hope for the day of a lot of rejoicing." He paused. "But in the meantime . . . we wait."

In Amish culture, you may be born into an Amish family, but you must choose for yourself if you want to be Amish. That usually happens somewhere between the ages of sixteen and twenty-one. This is the period called Rumspringa, when youth become more social and are given freedom to make choices for themselves. The term simply means "running around." Rumspringa varies greatly from community to community. Some smaller communities have almost no such wild youth. In larger communities, wild youth are much more common.

Eventually, though, all must choose: to stay and become baptized, or to leave.

As an Amish teen growing up in the 1970s, Ira Wagler described himself as "a hothead, strong willed, filled with passion and rage and desire. Stubborn. Driven." Ira ran around with five other boys—strong-willed boys who resisted whatever disciplinary actions the parents and preachers threw at them.

Ira left home for the first time when he was seventeen. "The first few times I left, I had every intention of returning and settling down," he said. "It wasn't even a question in my mind. Just a year or two, a taste of the outside, then I'd be content to live out my days in the Amish faith where I was born. Calm and settled in the simple life. Marry. Raise a family. Watch my children grow."

But it didn't happen that way for Ira. He seesawed back and forth—returning, leaving, returning. The last time Ira left, he got up in the middle of the night, scribbled a note to leave on his pillow, and never returned again.

Like Ira, Mose Gingerich waffled back and forth between leaving and staying Amish. Now in his late twenties, Mose is the ninth child in a family of thirteen. "My dad died when I was twelve. He was a strict Amish man who ruled his family with an iron fist. My mother never remarried, and my older brothers took over the father's role. I rebelled hard. I felt rebellion and resentment control me." He gave a short laugh. "I was branded as a black sheep early on. I just had a deep yearning to know what's out in the world. It would've been too dull for me to know only two hundred people, to only live on that farm."

When Mose turned sixteen, he left for the first time. He was the first to leave his family, the first to leave his small Amish community in Wisconsin. "But there were no other ex-Amish to hang out with in Wisconsin. I was lonesome, so I returned. Five years later, I left again. I knew I couldn't be Amish the rest of my life." Mose moved to Columbia, Missouri, where he found a community of formerly Amish. Like Ira, he has no regrets. "But I do miss the Amish lifestyle. I miss the community part—everyone pitches in and helps. You get in trouble, others drop everything to help. Among the Amish, everyone has each other's back."

Rachel Stutzman's teen years have been very tame compared to Ira's and Mose's. "I got to pick my own youth group," she said. "In my area, there are different ones, and they each have something unique. Some are open buggies, which are the most conservative. Some have a lot of parent supervision. Some allow boys to have cars. Usually it's the boys who have the cars, not the girls. I chose one because my older brothers and sisters went to this one and I knew the kids. They had younger brothers and sisters, so we were already friends. Girls bring desserts to a youth group—that's just a girl thing—and boys will bring beverages, and parents will provide pulled pork sandwiches and baked beans."

Through this youth group, Rachel met a special young man. Soon they will become baptized and marry. That is really the goal of Rumspringa, to affirm what is right and good about the Amish way of life. And to keep a young person spiritually home.

ROAD MAP: GETTING THERE FROM HERE

Amish or English, when a child rejects his parents' church, it is painful and troubling. "There's not a lot you can do about it," Samuel said. "Pray and be patient and be loving. And then we just wait." There is much to be gleaned from Samuel's response to Matthew: he prays for him, he works to keep a healthy and loving relationship, and he never gives up hope that his son will one day return to church.

Parenting has never been easy. But being a teenager isn't all that easy, either. In your life, what have been times of greatest growth and times of greatest struggle? Would you describe them as the same times?

The Amish have a saying, "If you can't change the past, don't ruin the present by worrying about the future." Worrying about what might happen to your teenager in the future does nothing but raise your anxiety level. Instead, try to be grateful for the present moment. Take things one day at a time. Remember Samuel's example: keep praying, keep loving, keep hoping.

In their own words...

My goal should never be to raise kids who make me look good. My goal should be to raise kids who love God and spend their lives honoring him.

—Scribe from Napanee, Indiana

On Friday evening our youth group sponsored and served a Valentine's supper to the married couples in church. They did a good job of decorating, cooking, and serving. I especially enjoyed the time after the meal when all the couples shared how they first met. Interesting, lots of awkward moments in the past! So a hint to young people now—if you feel awkward and uneasy, just remember that it's normal and part of life at that state. This too shall pass!

—Scribe from Danville, Ohio

Singing to Cora

Never lose sight of the fact that old age needs so little but it needs that little so much.

Amish Proverb

Cora Fisher loved hearing people sing hymns. Even as her dementia progressed, taking more and more of her mind, she enjoyed being sung to. She was 101 years old and lived in the same house she and her husband had bought as newlyweds. The same house where she had lived as a widow for forty-three years. Her granddaughter-in-law, Mary, took care of Cora. "Each morning when I went into her room, she asked me if I knew who she was," Mary said. "She didn't know who she was, and she had no idea who I was!"

Yet even as Cora's memories faded, her body stayed strong. "Over the years that we have been caring for her," Mary said, "it has been an eye-opener for us, knowing we are the next generation and what can happen to one's mind. We need to appreciate now what we so often take for granted, things like our memories."

Last July, Cora suffered a major stroke. "We knew the end would be near after that," Mary said. "What was interesting was that it seemed as if Cora knew too. She was very calm. It was as if she had totally given herself to God's will."

Within a week, Cora's body started to fail. "When I went to check on her on the morning that she died," Mary said, "her legs, nose, arms were turning purple. Hospice came to do her vitals and found both her respiratory and vascular systems were shutting down. Her heart was pounding, and breathing was labored. It was hard to see her suffer."

Mary was the first to notice when Cora's eyes flickered open. "Quickly we gathered as much family as we could around her bed. The children suggested singing, because that was Cora's most favorite thing of all. It was a special moment. Voices filled with emotions . . . or failed altogether . . . we sang such songs as *'Herrlich, Herrlich wird es einmal sein'* ('Joyful, Joyful Will the Meeting Be'). We were all with her when her soul took flight."

ROAD MAP: GETTING THERE FROM HERE

Mary took care of Cora right to the end—probably through some difficult years. And she wasn't even related by blood—she was Cora's granddaughter-in-law. The Amish provide a tremendous example of care and commitment to the elderly. Aging parents don't go to nursing facilities; they are cared for at home. Right to the end. Imagine the sense of security an elderly Amish person has, to be loved and valued, by their own family, right to the end.

Cora's grandchildren and great-grandchildren all gathered by her bedside to usher her into God's presence. Our modern culture prefers to avoid death scenes—especially in regard to children. Too emotional. Too unpleasant. Is that God's perspective? As Christians, we need not fear death. We do our children a great favor by facing death with calm and peace (see John 14:1–3; Ps. 23:4–6; 116:15).

Do your thoughts include much about heaven? The Bible tells us it is a real place one should be looking forward to! On a long car ride or at the dinner table one evening, start a conversation with your children about heaven. Ask them to imagine what it might be like. Study Scriptures to learn about it. After all, heaven is truly our home. "Joyful, joyful will the meeting be!"

In their own words . . .

It's been a long, cold winter, and I am eager for warm weather. I'm tired of seeing bare trees and lifeless brown leaves covering the ground. I long to see wildflowers poke through the dead leaves and to watch the woods turn green once more. Yet even as I anticipate my favorite season, I hear my mother's voice saying, "Don't wish your life away."

—Scribe from Windsor, Ohio

Myron has one uncle, Monroe M., who will be ninety-one on June 24. He can hardly see, but his mental running gears are pretty good. Wife Mattie, age eighty-eight, can see but is very hard of hearing and in a wheelchair, so between the two, one can hear and the other can see!

—Scribe from Winesburg, Ohio

Wedding Season

A happy marriage is a long conversation that always seems too short.

Amish Proverb

No one in Susanna Glick's extended family was surprised when they received word that she was planning to marry Ammon Fisher. "We'd heard that a certain young man from Lebanon County had been spying out the land and seemed to enjoy being in the presence of our Susanna an awful lot," said Sara Ellen Miller, Susanna's aunt, who lives in Indiana. Sara Ellen and her husband traveled back to Susanna's home in Lancaster County for the November wedding.

Traditionally, Amish weddings take place from late October through December, after the autumn harvest when the fields—and families—are resting. Weddings are held on Tuesdays and Thursdays, so there is time to prepare for the event and clean up after it.

A wedding is a particularly joyous occasion for the Amish. Two baptized members of the church join together, continue the faith, and a new family begins. These weddings are love matches; parents do not choose their child's mate, though approval must be given.

At a church service after fall communion, the couples planning to marry are "published"—announced in front of the congregation. But much preparation, mainly by the bride's parents, has already begun, including the planting in early summer of several hundred stalks of celery, an important part of any Lancaster Amish wedding feast. No one knows why! Like so many things about the Amish, celery is just . . . tradition. "That was another hint we had of a coming wedding," Sara Ellen said. "My sister had a huge patch of celery growing in her garden last summer."

The wedding service, held in the home of the bride's parents, is similar to the regular Sunday service. But the focus is on the serious step of marriage, for in the Amish church, there is no divorce. The sermons and Bible passages emphasize the relationship between man and wife. When it is time for the vows, the couple comes forward. Each is asked if they will remain together until death, and if they will be loyal and care for each other during adversity, affliction, sickness, and weakness. The minister then takes the couple's hands in his and, wishing them the blessing and mercy of God, tells them to "Go forth in the Lord's name. You are now man and wife."

"Susanna and Ammon's wedding was a true Lancaster-patterned wedding, with the long tables set up where the services had been," Sara Ellen said. "The weather was a perfect day, a blessing from our Lord." After the service, the benches used for the service are put together to form tables. During the wedding meal, the couple sits at the corner of two tables called the "Eck," with their attendants on each side, and the unmarried boys sitting opposite the girls.

Sara Ellen described the meal as a feast: roast chickens, stuffing (a mixture of bread and chicken), mashed potatoes, cole slaw, applesauce, and creamed celery. Some leafy celery stalks were also put in jars to decorate the table. Among the desserts were pies, doughnuts, fruit, and pudding. "There were several wedding cakes made by the women, but one from a bakery as well," Sara Ellen said. "They were eaten later in the day." She said it took several seatings to feed the three hundred plus guests. "I've been to weddings with over five hundred!"

In the afternoon, the young people had a singing. "Soon, it was time for the evening meal for those who had stayed through the day," Sara Ellen said. "And then comes the matchmaking!" Amish style, of course. The bride made a list of couples who were dating or interested in each other. As their names were called, they took their place at the table. More hymn singing followed the meal, with the "faster hymns" taking top billing. "Many, many young people caused the volume of hearty singing to rise and fall nonstop all afternoon, and then again after supper till midnight," Sara Ellen said. "If we would have had no other benefit it would've been worth all our efforts and expenses of traveling from Indiana just to listen to these songs of a spiritual wedding."

But it was what happened the next day that really made the trip worth every penny, she said. After spending the night at the bride's home, Susanna and Ammon woke the next day to begin helping with the cleanup from the day before. "In the afternoon, they started to open up some gifts," Sara Ellen said. "Ammon was handed a suspicious-looking box. He opened it carefully, first just enough to let the light in. Imagine everyone's surprise when a rooster popped its head out and started to crow! Everyone just howled. We still don't know who gave that gift. No one's admitting to it!"

Susanna and Ammon, like most Amish newlyweds, typically spend a few weekends visiting relatives before settling into their new life. "I'm not sure where that rooster is just now," Sara Ellen said. "My guess is Susanna will find a banty for it, and both rooster and hen will have a new home."

ROAD MAP: GETTING THERE FROM HERE

Weddings are such happy events! It's hard to imagine that one out of three couples marrying today will end up divorced. The next time you are invited to a wedding, consider adding that couple to your daily prayers.

Divorce is not an option for the Amish. They believe they are making a vow to God, not just to another person. Such a commitment would definitely encourage couples to work out their differences.

Most Christians would say that divorce is not an option, but the divorce rate is nearly the same for them as it is for mainstream Americans. Most marriages have a "shortcoming" or two. Or three! We all have gaps (Rom. 3:23). There will always be gaps in life on this side of heaven. God wants to reveal to you his ability to fill that gap in your marriage. Write out a prayer to God, telling him specifically what you want to achieve in your marriage. Be sure to tell him what you are willing to do to accomplish your desires.

Think of the long-term relationships in your life. How do you affirm them? Displaying your wedding photos is one simple way to show how you value your marriage vows. Or what about your business relationships? A California family buys coffee from a local coffee shop run by a Christian couple who are committed to the welfare of their town. There are all kinds of simple ways, easy ways, to honor commitment in your day-to-day life.

In their own words . . .

Brian and Rosie M. came home from their honeymoon to find some balloons in the house. Actually, make that a lot of balloons, with the bedroom and bathroom filled from floor to ceiling and some other rooms several feet deep. I understand this prank was incubated in the mind of Brian's uncle by marriage, Jason, who is otherwise a very sensible, conscientious man.

—Scribe from Grove City, Minnesota

A few girls are here helping us so I should get to work. We have the tables all in place and set over one hundred plates last evening. Now we have the porch and basement to do yet. It has been a busy week, but we still enjoyed it. On Wednesday, a whole gang of girls and some women helped us. The work just flew. It makes us feel so unworthy what everyone does for us. It is different for us since I don't have any parents to help us.

—Scribe from Shipshewana, Indiana

An Early Good-bye

Be life long or short, its completeness depends on what it was lived for.

Amish Proverb

After saving for years, David and Annie Schwartz bought their first farm in June. David had hoped they could have moved in earlier in spring, but the former owners wouldn't be hurried. He rushed to plant corn, wheat, and beans before the heat of summer arrived, working late into the evening. Annie worried about how hard he was driving himself, but she knew how much this farm meant to him. He was providing for his family—his wife, and his four-year-old son, Junior, and one-year-old daughter, Maggie.

Annie said it was the happiest summer of their lives. "As hard as David worked, he still made time for some fun family moments. One hot afternoon, he scooped up Junior and the two spent the rest of the day fishing. They caught no fish, but that's not the point of fishing anyhow, is it?" She smiled. "Happy, happy memories."

In August, David was loading hay into the haymow in the barn. Annie isn't quite sure what happened next, but she heard Junior screaming for her to come. She grabbed Maggie and rushed out to the field. She found her husband sprawled on the barn floor, unconscious.

David was taken by ambulance to the hospital in Wichita. Annie could tell, from the look on the faces of the paramedics, that David was in serious condition. At the hospital, she was told that he must have slipped and fallen from the haymow down to the concrete barn floor, landing on his head. His neck was broken. When she walked into David's room in the ICU, she felt as if she might pass out. "David was on a ventilator, with a machine doing the breathing for him." Only time would tell, the doctors told her, the extent of his paralysis.

One week passed. Then another. With a great deal of effort, David was able to communicate short words at a time. His mind was clear, of that Annie and the doctors had no doubt. She stayed at the hospital with him around the clock, and their family swept in and cared for Junior and Maggie. An aunt or uncle or grandparents brought the children to the hospital each day, stopping at a nearby Burger King for lunch. "The manager at Burger King heard about David's accident," Annie said, "and he wouldn't accept money anymore." She inhaled a deep breath. "So kind!"

They were just hanging on, one day at a time. "We were unsure of what the future held, but we knew who held our future," Annie said. "But at the end of the second week, David realized that the doctors didn't think he could live without the ventilator." She spoke slowly, out of the beautiful calm she seemed to wear like a coat. "He looked right at me for the longest time—I'll never forget that look. It was as if he was trying to tell me everything in that look—that he loved us, loved us so much, but that he couldn't live like this—and then he asked the doctors to take him off the ventilator."

Imagine trying to make such a heart-wrenching decision! Annie clasped her hands and leaned forward. "I didn't *want* to let him go. But I knew he was right. David was always busy, always bursting with energy. His mother used to say he was only completely still when he was sound asleep. I had to respect his wishes. It would have been selfish of me to hang on to him. He was ready to go."

The next morning, after David said his good-byes to his family, wife, and children, he was taken off the ventilator. His lung muscles were too paralyzed to work to breathe, so he labored hard to get air. His heart, though, was strong. The morning turned to afternoon, then to evening, then to another day. His entire extended family stayed by his bedside. Twenty-four hours and forty-five minutes after he was taken off the ventilator, David took his last breath. He was twenty-four years old. "It was David's time," Annie said confidently. Tears trickled from the corners of her eyes, but she didn't wipe them away. Instead, she let them fall. "His life was complete."

Road Map: Getting There from Here

Many Amish people say, after losing a loved one in an accident, not that the person was in the wrong place at the wrong time, but that they were in the *right* place at the *right* time. God is in control, they say, and it must have been that person's time to go to heaven. Do you believe that? Why or why not?

When a tragedy occurs, the first response of the Amish community is to always reach out, to show concern for how a person is coping, to come alongside and do everything they can to ease the person's grief. What has been helpful to you during a crisis? Make a point to share that same kind of help with someone else when they are in need.

We are not guaranteed a life free of pain or sorrow. Even amid hardship, trials, and things that don't go the way we want them to, we can find something to be joyful about. Annie said it best: "We were unsure of what the future held, but we knew who held our future." How does this perspective encourage you?

In their own words . . .

Yesterday was the funeral of my uncle John G. Late last Wednesday evening, John, age eighty-five, was taken home to be with his Lord. On my last visit with him about three weeks ago, he bravely stated his fearlessness of dying by saying, "I have cancer, but cancer doesn't have me." The prevailing mood of the funeral was one of joy and victory.

—Scribe from Uniontown, Ohio

A Circle of Life

To grow old gracefully, you must start when you are young.

Amish Proverb

Not a week goes by that Rose Graber doesn't spend time with her six grandchildren, all living within an hour's distance. "Being a grandparent, it's just the best!" Rose said. She has a pet poodle that she has trained to perform tricks. "The grandchildren love that dog. They like to come and see what new trick he can do." She's taught her dog to roll over, to sing (Woof! Woof!), to play dead when he hears the command "Dod!" and to identify which town the family lives in. "Do we live in Leola?" The dog remains still. "Do we live in Bird-in-Hand?" No response. "Do we live in Gordonville?" Woof! Rose gives her dog commands in Penn Dutch, because, of course, otherwise he would have to translate and it would take him longer.

Rose's warm brown eyes light up when she talks about her grandchildren. The integration of multiple generations within an Amish family is not simply endured—it is appreciated, nurtured, and cherished. Esteemed for their wisdom, the elderly find meaning and dignity as they assist their children. Surrounded by droves of grandchildren, they pass on the wisdom, joys, and secrets of Amish life to the rising generation.

"Having my folks around as I raise my children is a blessing," said Laura Mast, mother of four. "They not only help but they are giving my children a fine example of godly living. I just don't think children can have enough good examples."

Most Amish farmhouses have a Grossdaadi Haus. A young couple knows that someday their parents will pass on, and then they will move into the addition, the Grossdaadi Haus, and their children will take over the house. A circle of life.

Maiden aunts and bachelor uncles often live with extended family, either with elderly parents in the Grossdaadi Haus, or in small cottages tucked on the farm. Twins Emma and Edna grew up within shouting distance of their two maiden aunts. "Our own mother was so busy with seven kids and a household to run," Edna said. "The aunts had time for us. We used to go over each evening after dinner and spend time with the aunts. In a way, they were like having a second mother."

A fond memory for Ohio-born Katie Miller is that of her grandfather reading to her and her younger sisters on winter afternoons during off Sundays. "We would sit in front of the woodstove, and Grandpa would read to us stories from *Martyrs Mirror*. It was his way of teaching us, I suppose. He was a quiet man, not the kind of person who would ever tell you what to do, but he liked to show us, through stories, when we found ourselves in difficult situations." A perfect example of how the Amish influence younger generations: Katie's grandfather was weaving a rich culture deep into his granddaughters' way of thinking.

Extended families don't just live together, they often work together.

Amos Riehl runs a quilt shop with his wife, mother, and two daughters, in the bottom of his farmhouse in a small town near Lancaster, Pennsylvania. The quilt shop started accidentally. Amos is a farmer whose property wraps around an old abandoned public one-room schoolhouse. When the property was being auctioned off by the state of Pennsylvania, Amos grabbed it. "I didn't want that piece of property sold off to someone I didn't know." To help afford the taxes on that property, his wife offered to sell a quilt. First, though, the quilt top had to be quilted. A frolic was planned, and friends and neighbors pitched in to help. The quilt sold for enough to pay for the first year's taxes. At that point, Amos's church felt that they could use the schoolhouse for their own children. Amos sold the property to the church for a loss. "If there's one thing you can guarantee about the Amish, it's that they won't allow anyone in their community to go it alone." Women of all ages started to help make quilt tops on a regular basis to help the Riehls weather that financial contribution. It wasn't long until a cottage business developed for the Riehls. The quilt shop grew so quickly that Amos stepped in as manager and let his sons-in-law farm their many acres.

Two little impish boys peeked through a dusty basement window and waved at Amos, their grandfather. One of the boys had a chocolate milk mustache. Amos shook his head at the boys. "What I like about having grandchildren is that you can have fun with them." He points a big thumb up to the main house where his daughter and son-in-law live. "But the best part is when they start getting queer [tired, unhappy], you can send them back."

ROAD MAP: GETTING THERE FROM HERE

Changes in family structure are inevitable. Our nests fill up and then empty out in the blink of an eye. The Amish seem to accept and prepare for change right from the beginning, rather than mourning or dreading it. What are some benefits of the Amish attitude toward change?

The presence of the older generation is not simply tolerated in an Amish home; it is appreciated, valued, cherished. Try to find a way to incorporate the value of older people in your family life. One Montana mom invited her newly widowed grandmother to move in. A Pennsylvania family stops by a retirement home after church to visit a former neighbor. One young woman visits her grandfather's Alzheimer's facility and plays well-loved hymns on the piano. It's important to show the elderly people in your life that you haven't forgotten them.

Aunts, uncles, and grandparents can be extremely influential in younger generations. It takes effort, though, to build an ongoing relationship with a child. You have to be the one who reaches out—a child can't be expected to take the initiative. Is there a relative in your life with whom you could develop a closer relationship? Send an email, remember a birthday, pick up the phone and call. Do something to show you care!

Cousins can be as close as siblings. They need time together to create memories and share their lives. What are some ways you can foster the relationship between your children and your nieces/nephews? Remember, loving relationships take time and nurturing. And someone to make the effort.

In their own words . . .

Thank you, Lord, that I have a few things worth giving. Even if it's a lap to be sat on or the comfort of a warm embrace.

—Scribe from Seymour, Missouri

After retiring from dairying in 1994, I started to help my wife, Rachel, piece quilt tops. I find I enjoy helping her. A friend said he hasn't stooped that low yet. But I still call him a friend.

—Scribe from Somerset, Pennsylvania

Epilogue

An Evening of Trivial Pursuit with the Amish

*Kindness is a language which the deaf can hear and the blind
can see.*

Amish Proverb

While in Pennsylvania researching this book, I was invited by an Amish friend to attend her family's Trivial Pursuit party. During the winter months, this family has a monthly gathering of friends: mostly Amish, some Mennonites, a handful of English. Ruth, my friend, is the heart of this collection of friends. She is warm and outgoing, loving and nonjudgmental. Ruth's friends adore her, it's plain to see.

We spent the day getting supplies for the party: ice cream, juice, popcorn, and some ingredients for an unusual treat that Ruth called "bachelor hats." Back at home, she layered a Ritz cracker with peanut butter, then cut a marshmallow in half and stuck it on the peanut butter. A few minutes under the broiler, and the "bachelor hats" truly look like little Amish straw hats . . . minus the black band.

Ruth's grown sons helped clear the furniture out of the family room and set up two long tables and folding chairs. Ruth was busy popping popcorn and laying it out on large baking sheets. She salted it lightly, then drizzled melted chocolate over the popcorn and set the trays in the basement to harden.

At seven in the evening, buggies started arriving. A few cars, too. Within a few minutes, the room was full with moms, dads, babies, toddlers. Older children slipped down into the large finished basement to play Ping-Pong. These people knew the Trivial Pursuit drill. They got right to work. Men on one table, women on the other. It's the same edition of the game that we play in our home. The only change they made was to use Bible trivia questions to replace Arts and Entertainment questions. Fair enough.

I took my seat and hoped all of my synapses were firing. I used to be pretty good at this game, but I knew enough about the Amish to know that this would be a challenge. These people were readers, and their minds were refreshingly uncluttered from TV and movies. Their memory for detail always astounded me.

It wasn't long before I shook my head in wonder. Both sides—men and women—answered questions correctly that I couldn't even wrap my head around. "Which two colleges played the first football game?" "Princeton and Rutgers!" And oh my . . . they knew their Bible! Though the men had a "ringer," the bishop, they didn't have to rely on him. "Which queen in the Bible did away with her grandchildren?" While I assumed Jezebel (wrong!), someone else called out, "Queen Athaliah!" (right!).

Ruth quietly worked around the table, passing around bowls of chocolate-drizzled popcorn, bachelor hats, potato chips, and a beverage of orange soda. Nothing fancy, but delicious and game-friendly.

But here's what really stood out to me: their kindness.

If the same event—a board game of men versus women—were happening in my home (and I don't think my home is unique in this), competitiveness would reign supreme. "It wouldn't be long before insults would be zinging across the table in my home!" said one friend as I explained the evening to him. How often, in your home, has a family night of games ended when one sibling rushes out of the room in tears because he lost, or because something hurtful was said by another sibling?

In this Amish home, kindness reigned. The men gave the women plenty of time to think out a question. There was no buzzer to time a team out. When someone answered a question correctly, compliments and approving raised eyebrows abounded. Babies were passed between moms and dads. Children ran up to the table to whisper something to a parent, then they would quietly disappear again to play. Jokes were gentle and good-natured, with plenty of belly laughs. But no cutting remarks or sarcasm were fired off. Not *one!* The Amish foster a culture of kindness.

When the game was over (after a nail-biter finish, the men won), families helped clean up and put things away. And then they all thanked Ruth and left in their buggies or cars to head home in the dark. Happy and satisfied after an evening of fun and fellowship, just as it was meant to be.

It's a shame that kindness is almost rendered meaningless in our culture. It isn't modeled much. Just the opposite. At times, I think the popularity of reality television has to do with a pleasure we take in meanness, in seeing someone humiliated. The more sarcastic, the ruder the comments, the more drawn in we get. Would *American Idol* have soared in popularity without Simon Cowell's acerbic tongue? Someone said, it's like all of America attended Smart-mouth College.

The Amish relate to each other differently. Kindness first. It's a simple concept, but it's not always easy to implement at home. Yet kindness can change dynamics in relationships: between husband and wife, between parent and child, between siblings.

Sound too simple? A study at Kenyon College conducted a test in cooperation with the US Navy to find out how the tone of the voice affected sailors when they were given orders. The conclusion found that the way a person was addressed determined the kind of response he would make. When a sailor was spoken to in a soft voice, he would answer in a similar manner. But when he was shouted at, he shouted back.

What we say and how we say it not only makes a difference in the reaction we'll receive, but it also determines whether conflict or peace will result. "A soft answer turns away wrath, but a harsh word stirs up anger" (Prov. 15:1 NKJV).

In a world where callous thoughtlessness and selfish indifference are all too common, kindness can transform lives. When our walk harmonizes with our words of witness, simple kindness can make a compelling impact on others by pointing them to the type of love God has for them in Jesus Christ. What a difference such kindness can make in our homes, our neighborhoods, our schools, our churches, our communities! But *especially* in our homes.

Why be kind? There's no better reason than because that is how God treats us (Eph. 4:32).

Recommended Reading

I f you are interested in learning about Amish life and beliefs, these nonfiction publications will give you an accurate picture of what it means to be born Plain.

The Budget
PO Box 249
Sugarcreek, OH 44681
Published weekly

A Joyful Chaos blog by Mary Ann Kinsinger
www.ajoyfulchaos.blogspot.com.

The Riddle of Amish Culture by Donald B. Kraybill (The Johns Hopkins University Press, 1989).

Success Made Simple: An Inside Look at Why Amish Businesses Thrive by Erik Wesner (Jossey-Bass, 2010).

20 Most Asked Questions about the Amish and Mennonites by Merle and Phyllis Good (Good Books, 1995).

An Amish Paradox: Diversity and Change in the World's Largest Amish Community by Charles E. Hurst and David L. McConnell (The Johns Hopkins University Press, 2010).

The Amish Way: Patient Faith in a Perilous World by Donald B. Kraybill, Steven M. Nolt, and David L. Weaver-Zercher (Jossey-Bass, 2010).

Country Lane Quilts and Family Cooking by Katie, Barbie, and Kathryn Stoltzfus (self-published through Whitmore Printing, 2007). To order copies:
Country Lane Quilts
221 South Groffdale Road
Leola, Pennsylvania 17540

Notes

Introduction

1. Findings taken from the following sources: Jared R. Anderson and William J. Doherty, "Democratic Community Initiatives: The Case of Overscheduled Children," *Family Relations*, vol. 54 (Dec. 2005): 655; http://www.aboutourkids. org/articles/family_meals_matter%E2%80%94staying_connected; http://www.usa today.com/life/lifestyle/2010-04-15-1Afamilytime15_CV_N.htm; and http://www. digitalcenter.org/pages/recent_findings_content.asp?intGlobalId=61&intTypeId=2.

Section One Children Are Loved but Not Adored

1. Erik Wesner, *Success Made Simple: An Inside Look at Why Amish Businesses Thrive* (San Francisco: Jossey-Bass, 2010).

2. Cheryl Harner, *Weedpicker's Journal: Cheryl's Flora and Fliers* (blog), http://www.flora-quest.com/blogpage.html.

3. Bruce Glick, "Christmas Bird Counts in Ohio's Amish Country," *American Birds*, http://www.audubon.org/bird/cbc/pdf/AB_107_04-glick.pdf.

4. Bruce Glick, "Christmas Bird Counts in Ohio's Amish Country," *The 107th Christmas Bird Count: American Birds*, National Audobon Society, vol. 61, 2006–2007, 29; http://www.audubon.org/bird/cbc/pdf/AB_107_04-glick.pdf.

Section Two Great Expectations

1. Sheba R. Wheeler, "College 101 for Parents: The Balancing Art of Being Involved and Letting Go," *Denver Post*, August 11, 2010, http://www.denverpost.com/lifestyles/ci_15661354.

2. "2009 College Graduates Moving Back Home in Larger Numbers," *College Grad.com*, July 22, 2009, http://www.collegegrad.com/press/2009_college_graduates _moving_back_home_in_larger_numbers.shtml.

3. Sharon Jayson, "It's Time to Grow Up—Later," *USA Today*, September 30, 2004, http://www.usatoday.com/life/lifestyle/2004-09-30-extended-adolescence_x. htm.

4. "New Marriage and Divorce Statistics Released," Barna Group, March 31, 2008, http://www.barna.org/barna-update/article/15-familykids/42-new -marriage-and-divorce-statistics-released.

5. Personal email correspondence with Erik Wesner.

Section Four Letting Go

1. "The Barna Group reported in 2006 that 61 percent of young adults who had attended church as teenagers were now spiritually disengaged, not participating in worship or spiritual disciplines. A year later, LifeWay Research released similar findings, that seven in ten Protestants ages 18–30 who had worshiped regularly in high school stopped attending church by age 23." Leslie Leyland Fields, "The Myth of the Perfect Parent," *Christianity Today*, January 8, 2010, http://www. christianitytoday.com/ct/2010/january/12.22.html.

Suzanne Woods Fisher is the author of *The Choice, The Waiting*, and *The Search*—the bestselling Lancaster County Secrets series. Her grandfather was raised in the Old Order German Baptist Brethren Church in Franklin County, Pennsylvania. Her interest in living a simple, faith-filled life began with her Dunkard cousins.

Suzanne is also the author of *Amish Peace: Simple Wisdom for a Complicated World*, a finalist for the ECPA Book of the Year award, and *Amish Proverbs: Words of Wisdom from the Simple Life*. She is the host of "Amish Wisdom," a weekly radio program on toginet. com. She lives with her family in the San Francisco Bay Area and raises puppies for Guide Dogs for the Blind. To Suzanne's way of thinking . . . you just can't take life too seriously when a puppy is tearing through your house with someone's underwear in its mouth.

You can find Suzanne online at www.suzannewoodsfisher.com.

Make the Peace and Wisdom of the Amish a Reality in Your Life

Simple Wisdom *for a* Complicated World

Amish Peace

Suzanne

Amish Proverbs

Words of Wisdom from the Simple Life

Suzanne Woods Fisher

Meet

SUZANNE WOODS FISHER

Visit her website
www.SuzanneWoodsFisher.com

Friend her on  Suzanne Woods Fisher

Follow her on Suzannewfisher

Listen to her on the popular internet radio show
Amish Wisdom, now available for free download from iTunes.